Here!

Immigrant and Refugee Youth Through the Eyes of Their Middle School Teacher

ANN C. SMITH

Testimonials

Here! offers a glimpse into the real world of an ESL classroom. "Quality teaching outweighs the benefit of any other resource." Ms. Smith makes a compelling case for small classes and direct English language acquisition instruction. Her forthright, heartfelt, and sometimes humorous stories also convey the impact a teacher can make with an emotional connection and commitment to do what is needed.

— **Susan Wall, M.Ed., Educator**

Ann Smith's stories do a wonderful job of depicting young American immigrants' spirit of resilience and determination. I fell in love with many of the book's personalities.

— **Bella Magallon Alex, Retired Program Administrator,**
Texas Department of Family and Protective Services,
Child Protective Services Division

Ann Smith threads together instances (in and out of the classroom, no matter how fleeting) of comic relief, bonding, and especially the continuous challenges she encountered teaching immigrant and refugee middle-school kids. And what are those challenges? Coming-of-age issues like peer pressure, of course. But also assimilation, family separation and disconnect, dropping out and truancy, illiteracy and language acquisition. And all of these are magnified because each young person experiencing them is a stranger in a strange land.

— **Dixie Binford, Administrative Specialist for School Improvement,**
Texas Education Service Center Region 13

Ann C. Smith's *Here!* is funny, heartwarming, and thought-provoking. Her masterful storytelling supersedes educational dogma and gives validation to students and teachers, all of whom need a brighter pathway for learning.

— **Tina Roberts, M.Ed., ESL Educator,**
Pickle Elementary (Dual Language School),
Austin Independent School District

A wise and humorous look into our secondary educational system that reveals challenges faced by immigrant students and their teachers today. These challenges—but, more importantly, the victories of Ann Smith's students—come alive in vivid detail, and they connect us to a world unfamiliar to many. The book is at once timely, timeless, and loving.

— **Michelle Le Brun, Producer/Director, *Death: A Love Story***
(Nominated for the Grand Jury Prize, Sundance Film Festival 1999)
Adjunct Professor, Harrington School of
Communication and Media, University of Rhode Island

About the Author

Ann C. Smith holds a master's degree in Teaching English as a Second Language from the Experiment in International Living's School for International Training. She had a thirty-year run as an ESL teacher mainly in Texas middle schools. She now lives in Austin with her partner and her son.

Here!

Immigrant and Refugee Youth Through the Eyes of Their Middle School Teacher

ANN C. SMITH

2020

JANUS IMPRINTS

First Edition

228 Pages

ISBN (print): 979-8-566593-41-8

Library of Congress Control Number: 2020923750

Printed under the imprimitur Janus Imprints by Dr. Jeremiah P. Spence at Austin, Texas, in the United States of America

Cover art prepared by Mark McConachie

This text edited by Ike West and Susan Luton

Dedication

In loving memory of my parents, Valerie and Howard Smith—second- and third-generation Americans respectively, idealists, faith leaders, community builders. Fortunate to have reaped the economic benefits of the post-World War II era, they believed in their country and strove to make it better for everyone within its borders.

Acknowledgments

I now know that it takes a village to write a book. With that said, I would like to first thank my two editors (and authors themselves), Ike West and Susan Luton. They each came to the book under serendipitous circumstances. Ike, a neighbor I met at a yoga class at our local library, is ten years my senior and fifty years wiser. Willing to overlook my lack of experience as a writer because she found the "cores" of my stories moving and relevant to current events, she painstakingly red-inked again and again several chapters over the course of nine months. We exchanged documents on my front porch as she passed by on her nightly walks, she with flashlight in hand. I slowly began to acquire some writing skills.

Later, when it came time for another round of revisions, I felt that what I most needed was an editor who had also been a public school language teacher. Knowing that the odds of locating such a person were slim, I ran my cursor down a long list of editors supplied by the Texas Writers League. I landed it somewhere in the middle on a female name that appealed to me for some reason. Within an hour, I had made contact with not only a fantastic editor but one who had taught bilingual education in the Austin Independent School District: Susan Luton! Both women were true collaborators and coaches who believed in me and in this project. Without their talent, hard work, and attention to detail, the book would be of a decidedly different caliber.

Secondly, I would like to thank my publisher, Dr. Jeremiah Spence, Visiting Professor at The University of Texas at Austin and an author as well, who publishes under the imprimatur "Janus Imprints" in Austin, Texas, utilizing the KDP Publishing-On-Demand platform. We too crossed paths in fortuitous circumstances: he was a friend of a friend. His passion and creative suggestions added immensely to the finishing touches and presentation.

I am forever grateful for the hundreds of students who I'll always hold in fond memory, and for the many colleagues who mentored and empowered me throughout a hard but fulfilling career. Also, *muchas gracias* to my friends who listened to my ongoing anguish and encouraged me every step of the way toward my dream of becoming an author.

Finally, I want to give a big shout-out to my family: to my son, Mateer Hudgens, who so often sweetly tolerated a preoccupied mom and who hesitantly allowed me to include him in my stories; and to Tommy Sutton, my better half, who, although he reads fishing tales almost exclusively, has always lovingly insisted that this book will be a bestseller.

Preface

Throughout my teaching career, I'd sometimes tell stories about a classroom situation or a memorable interaction with my students. Once in a great while, a listener would remark, "Ann, you should write a book." I must have held that thought.

On an early November morning, months into my retirement, I woke up feeling disillusioned. Out of sorts. The previous night a candidate I'd worked hard for had lost an election. Gazing at the ceiling, I asked myself, *What now?*

I had no plan in mind—not even an intention. And yet my legs marched me to the office at the back of the house. I sat down and started to write what, six years later, became this book. The writing journey was arduous and soul-searching. But in the very beginning on that fateful November morning, and for several days afterward, the ideas magically flowed. (That's a good thing. If I'd understood what lay ahead of me, I probably wouldn't have bothered.) In my heart, I believe the project transpired in the way it did because it was meant to be.

Ultimately, I like to think of this book as my version of a tribute to immigrant and refugee students and their courage, but also to educators in urban public schools, where the landscape is often impacted by so many households in poverty or near poverty. I've worn other hats in my adult years, pre- and post-teaching: grassroots organizer, canvasser, social worker, parent, caretaker, writer. None of these have come close to public school educator in terms of the various and subtle skills required, the stress endured, and the great but not frequent rewards gained.

You might ask why I became an ESL (English as a Second Language) teacher. I know of two principal reasons, the first but less significant one being *my lifelong fascination with language.* When I was a kid, I'd pretend to speak French or Italian or pig Latin with my friends on a city bus or in an ice-cream shop. Other times I'd pretend to be deaf and make up sign language symbols. When I was in college, I took philology and loved it. (If I'd been more of an academic, I would have chosen linguistics as a field of study.) I enjoy observing how people acquire language, and speculating how language itself evolves.

The more significant reason has to do with *a unique childhood experience.* In 1966 my parents, who were civil rights activists, moved our white family from New England to Chicago's South Side. There, my father's job involved race and housing issues—namely, to prevent white flight to Chicago's suburbs. From first through fifth grades, formative years, I lived in a predominantly Black community. My friends and neighbors were exclusively Black. I identified with the culture and wanted desperately to fit in. Then in 1970 my family moved back to New England, specifically to the lily-white town of West Hartford, Connecticut. I was in culture shock. It might as well have been another country. My yearning, at the age of ten, to return to Chicago was very, very painful. I fantasized about running away, and for the next two years I dreamed of the South Side. I've often wondered whether this part of my childhood allowed me to empathize with young people's feelings of wanting to assimilate into (or resist) a different culture—and also of sorely missing a place they were forced to leave behind forever.

I grew up in cities and towns in the North, but my official public school career took root in Texas. I first worked at a middle school in Houston, from 1990 to 2000. The school was primarily Black, with an immigrant population I'd guesstimate to be twenty or thirty students in any given year. From 2000 to 2014, I worked at a middle school in Austin that also housed a magnet program. The population was more diverse, but the majority of students were Latinx. The LEP (Limited English Proficient) population was large—approaching 50 percent.

Some points of clarification may be needed. In education circles, *immigrant students* refers to those who have resided in the United States for three or fewer consecutive years. *LEP (Limited English Proficient)* students are those who enter U.S. schools not speaking English as their primary language and have a limited ability to comprehend, speak, read, or write English. They maintain this label until they reach a certain standard of English proficiency. Not all LEP students are immigrants; yet immigrant students are generally LEP, unless they enter the United States speaking fluent English (which isn't often the case). In this book, I designate my students as *ESL (English as a Second Language)* rather than LEP, because I think the public is more familiar with the former term. Also, when I began my career, I was an ESL teacher hired to teach ESL classes—despite the fact that many of my students weren't acquiring English as a second language but rather as a third or even fourth one. As an aside, during my years of teaching, ESL morphed into *ESOL (English for Speakers of Other Languages)*, to *ELL (English Language Learner)*, and presently to *multilingual learner*.

Portable, when used to describe a space on a school campus, is a mobile-home version of a classroom. During some of the years I worked at the Austin school, I taught in a portable.

Of the chapters set in the Austin school (which make

17

up the greater part of the book), a few students and staff members appear in more than one of them. Despite this, no chapter is a prerequisite for understanding any chapters that follow.

Finally, all names have been changed to protect people's privacy, except for my dog's and, of course, my own.

Out of the Mouths of Babes

Three girls sat in the back of my minivan. Legs of varying lengths and shapes lined the seat. The smell of Pantene and other hair products permeated the car.

These three students of mine had stayed after school ostensibly to help clean, but more likely to hang with each other. They'd spent several minutes washing the whiteboard and sweeping my classroom floor, which the custodian appreciated. But soon they were entertaining themselves with a blaring boombox, seeing who could come up with the silliest dance routine. I'd agreed beforehand to drive them home, and this had also served as a motivator for staying later. Who could blame the girls for wanting to avoid the noisy school bus or the stop-and-go of the city bus after a long day?

Our first stop after leaving the campus was my son's daycare a few blocks away. They didn't even notice, being completely consumed with their animated conversation, interwoven with laughter and teasing, that had begun in the classroom. In fact, they were oblivious to anything except the satisfaction that comes from spending free time with friends.

Soon my shy four-year-old climbed into the back seat, landing in a sea of limbs and backpacks. His tangled mass of golden locks contrasted with the long dark strands of freshly brushed hair.

The girls squealed in adoration as they helped Jonas get strapped into his booster seat.

"Oh, Ms. Smith. She so little."

"Pretty hair."

"I love her eyes."

In their early stage of language acquisition, my students confused pronouns. Hopefully, Jonas hadn't picked up on their errors.

One of the girls squeezed his cheek gently. *"Ay, qué lindo. ¿Cómo te llamas?"* She wanted to know my beautiful boy's name. The other girls cooed and giggled.

We meandered through back streets in the general direction of their homes. I'd chosen today's route because it was safer. Slower too, which I welcomed after the harried pace of the school day. With the windows down, the late afternoon air felt warm but not hot. All in all, a perfect moment.

The girls and I chitchatted in Spanish. They knew I welcomed opportunities to speak their language, especially away from the classroom. It was the start of the school year, and soon enough the English of these young students would surpass my Spanish—and my chances to practice it would diminish.

Suddenly they alerted me.

"¿Qué pasó, hijito?" One of the girls had asked my son, her voice heavy with concern, what was wrong.

"Ms. Smith, *está llorando.*" I looked in my rearview mirror. Jonas *had* teared up. This surprised me. Ordinarily, he didn't show much emotion.

"What's the matter, Jonas?" I asked.

"I don't understand what they're saying," he said between hiccups, trying not to break down. "And you're talking just like them."

"Okay, girls. Let's speak in English," I announced.

20

"You need to practice anyway."

So they counted Jonas's toes and attempted a version of "This Little Piggy." Before long, they started reciting the Halloween poem they'd learned in class that morning: "Five little punkins sittin' in a gate. First one say, 'Hurry, don' be late.'"

I smiled to myself.

Eventually they got bored, as teens do, and reverted to Spanish with each other. Jonas, relieved to no longer be the center of attention, made engine sounds for the toy truck he pushed back and forth along the edge of the seat.

During his daycare years, Jonas spent many after-school hours with my students, sometimes in our minivan, sometimes visiting destinations close to the school, sometimes in my classroom. He saw bigger and browner boys than he sprinting in and out of my portable. Sweaty and pumped up from their last-period athletics class, my soccer students passed the twenty-minute break between school and team practice in the portable. They jumped on beanbags, rolled, wrestled, and swore, all in playful jest. Occasionally they gave Jonas gentle attention. They high-fived him, tousled his hair, called him "homey." Then they'd turn to chasing each other round and round the perimeter of the pushed-together student tables, grabbing random chairs and spinning them to trip each other up, narrowly avoiding ramming into bookcases. Jonas would intently observe their sporadic movements and whirlwind energy. Despite their rowdiness, they were good kids. Still, I'd listen eagerly for the soccer coach's distant whistle, a signal to get to the field. When the sound finally slipped in through the open door, the boys would leap to their feet and, within seconds, all energy was zapped from the room.

"Chao, niño," they'd say, patting Jonas on the shoulder.

"Bye, Miss. See you tomorrow!" a few would always holler on the way out. One boy might abruptly pull the door closed to prevent his buddy from an easy exit. A door tug-of-war would ensue until I yelled for them to stop. The two would immediately retreat, the door would slam shut—and then complete silence, leaving my ears buzzing. Before going home, Jonas and I would restore order among the overturned chairs, unaligned tables, and displaced blackboard erasers.

Jonas's interactions with my students became less frequent once he entered public school. And his academic experience turned out to be very different from that of my students. He attended schools in a suburban community of Austin that had one of the highest average household incomes in the state. Throughout his school years, he possibly knew of a handful of immigrant students enrolled in his district. They'd entered having already learned English in their countries of origin. And if they hadn't, their parents hired expert tutors once they arrived. The ESL population hovered around the 50 percent mark in any given year at my school, located in the Austin Independent School District, and this population qualified for free lunch. Actually the vast majority of the entire student body qualified for free lunch, and because of this the school received Title 1 government funding.

In my efforts to succeed with my students, I often felt frustrated by the district's seeming disregard for immigrant students' needs. Any concerns about English as a *Second* Language truly did get treated as *secondary*. I wondered why the powers that be didn't allocate the necessary time and resources for middle school and high school students to learn English. District-wide trainings tended to target literacy or math and science skills. Language acquisition? Not so much.

I tried to make sense of this disregard. State legislators' fears of a lack of public support for immigration issues, or their own lack of concern, seemed to be contributing factors. I sensed an unspoken perception, a clinging to the belief, that the immigrant tradition—part of the American dream—should never involve making allowances. Previous immigrant groups had climbed the economic ladder, had become American citizens, without special educational programs. Americans seemingly wanted to glorify the immigrant's struggle to assimilate.

Whatever the rationale for the inattention, the high school dropout rate of ESL students exceeded the national average. In many cases, a major reason for high failure rates on state-mandated exams at an urban secondary school in the United States was that a large portion of the students consisted of ESL learners. To me, the failure problem and the solution lay in the instruction. Ever since my days in graduate school, I'd carried close to my heart a theory upheld by linguists: the age of twelve is the general turning point in brain development, after which a human requires *explicit* instruction in acquiring a new language. Yet I was being pressured by the higher-ups not to teach explicitly, but instead to follow the core language arts curriculum *and intertwine* language objectives as they surfaced. Language acquisition (and its instruction) was neither intensive nor encouraged as the focus. In truth, it seemed an afterthought.

Jonas witnessed firsthand the differences between his academic community and mine. His early exposure to my students and school setting had ultimately given him a certain insight. That insight proved helpful to me in a moment of despair.

It was an afternoon in early spring. I was taking him, now a sixth-grader and playing soccer himself, to practice. With newly released test scores dominating my brain—I could think of nothing else—I dared to pose a question. "Jonas, why do you think 88 percent of the sixth-graders in your school scored 'commended' on the TAKS reading test, while 43 percent of the sixth-graders in my school barely passed? Why are the scores so lopsided?" Assuming the subject wouldn't hold his interest, I glanced sideways to check whether I was even on his radar.

Looking straight ahead, he considered the question. I braced for a brutal, juvenile response: *Students at your school don't listen to the teachers.* Or, *the kids at your school don't care about learning.* Or, worse yet, *the teachers at your school aren't very good.*

Instead, Jonas said, "Maybe because at your school a lot of kids don't speak English very well."

His response, simple and spot-on, led me to reclaim a singleness of purpose. A renewed commitment to effectively teach my students the English language. It rescued me from my confused state caused by working in a complex system that pulled me in too many directions. I also reclaimed my belief that, as a trained educator, I was the most viable advocate for my students' academic needs.

In the years to come, I would often struggle to maintain that singleness of purpose and the confidence to be that advocate for my ESL learners. Yet on that afternoon of my son's response, these became, and were to remain, worthy goals.

Skate(board)

Soe Lin made his initial entry into my ESL portable one misty November morning. The weather had been dreary for a few days. (On the plus side, though, in general the dreariness did help to create a mood of relative focus and productivity.) The direct instruction segment of the lesson had just ended, and students were preparing to write an assignment. As usual, a flurry of activity erupted when students reconfigured their work areas.

"My pencil. Somebody take my pencil." Miguel Ángel often accused his classmates of petty theft to avoid getting started.

Magaly arranged the work area to better assist the three new Guatemalans who had arrived only weeks before.

"Come, Marta. Sit," Lupe bossed her friend sitting across the room. "I need help. Please." Ignoring Lupe's petitions, Marta lifted her paper to view it at closer range.

A bit on edge until everyone got settled, I deliberately slowed down. I told myself that transitions involving twenty middle-schoolers necessarily took time.

Eventually the frenzy subsided. I sat at my desk to take attendance, basking in the quiet.

Then came a knock on the door. *What now?* I grumbled to myself.

Rafael, closest to the door, leaned sideways from his seat and slammed the metal lever downward. The door popped open and in walked two students, a familiar office assistant followed by a tiny boy. The assistant marched to my desk and handed me papers, while the small stranger stood shyly at the back of the classroom. All eyes turned toward him. He was cute, with chubby cheeks and dimples and a broad smile displaying an array of jagged teeth. His straight jet-black hair stuck up like porcupine quills. I assumed he was entering sixth grade, although he could have easily been taken for a fourth-grader.

"Welcome to the class," I said, making an even greater than usual effort to speak slowly and clearly. "Where are you from?"

He continued to smile, nodding his head. He hadn't understood me.

I skimmed the paperwork: *First Name: Soe. Last Name: Lin. Nationality: Burmese. Country of Origin: Thailand. Language: Burmese. Grade: 6.*

The office assistant quickly exited. *He's all yours,* his footsteps seemed to echo.

Suddenly, I felt abandoned and wished for any job but mine. *How will I ever catch him up?* I thought, as a familiar panic set in.

Then, turning away from my own comparatively trivial concerns, I tried putting myself in the shoes of this small child. He'd just set foot in an American classroom for the first time in his life and didn't speak a lick of English. I gestured for him to sit with Noé, an older student with a reassuring demeanor and a willingness to help. And yet, to be honest, my resentment of the untimeliness of this newcomer's arrival, and of others who had preceded him, lingered.

Finally, with an inaudible sigh, I gave in to the situation. I would forgo the day's writing activity.

"Everybody, stop what you're doing," I announced.

"Let's form a circle around Soe Lin and introduce ourselves. You can finish your work later." Wistfully I watched Magaly and Rafael lift their chairs, eyes still on their work, then obediently carry them to sit close to the newest member of the group.

Taking turns, each student gave a first name and a favorite food or activity.

"My name is Liliana," the first one began in her deliberate voice. "I'm from Mexico and I like study English."

Next it was Sylvie's turn. She giggled through her entire intro, taking twice as long as Liliana and threatening to stall the entire drill. None of us, let alone Soe Lin, could understand her. But her silliness proved contagious and Soe Lin broke into laughter. I relaxed, knowing his pleasant temperament would serve him well in the months ahead.

Soe Lin was academically as far behind as a student could be. He recited and read the English alphabet, something taught in refugee camps in Thailand. That was the extent of his literacy. His first language, one of fifty tribal languages in Burma (or Myanmar, as the country is also called), had no written form. He hadn't learned English phonics, and his pronunciation was unintelligible. He needed a one-on-one Burmese bilingual tutor, but I was all he had. I would be his teacher for the duration of his middle-school experience. I had to trust that within those three years, he'd become proficient enough in English to function at a basic level of listening, speaking, reading, and writing before moving on to high school.

In the beginning, I granted Soe Lin certain freedoms to minimize his frustration and my own. He copied from other students' work whenever he chose to. On the rare occasion when I asked him to respond, he'd decline by shaking his head. I didn't press. He seemed content to plod along. One pleasant surprise: he stayed focused.

Weeks later, Soe Lin's situation improved when two more Burmese students joined the class. Slightly older, they were boy and girl cousins. I watched as their brows furrowed while they took copious notes. The margins in their personal notebooks filled with neat and intricate Burmese words, their Burmese-English dictionaries always within reach. But neither notes nor dictionaries helped Soe Lin. It was his compatriots' role-modeling that did the trick. He observed how at ease they performed in a school setting, and how determined they were to acquire information.

The Burmese students came to form a threesome. Politely, without disrupting others, the two cousins explained vocabulary to Soe Lin through artful sketches and quiet discussions. Now that he was under their direction, I continued to let his progress take shape with little guidance from me.

For months, he averaged spelling two out of ten words correctly on his biweekly tests. I feigned delight in the two words and disregarded the eight errors. "Yes, that's right, Soe Lin. You understand. You *are* learning English," I'd cheer, exaggerating how pleased I was whenever he showed any inkling of comprehension.

Soe Lin never gave up.

In the second semester of his second year, fifteen months after his arrival, Soe Lin stunned us all with an unexpected and uncharacteristic outburst. It changed his reputation forever. On that February afternoon, I still hadn't heard him freely utter a complete sentence. His speech had remained monosyllabic, while his literacy had progressed to spelling five out of ten tested words correctly. He could read a simple paragraph fluidly, yet he didn't understand what he'd read.

On the day of his life-changing pronouncement, there was a weekly class competition to review vocabulary. Fourteen students, divided into two teams, sat in a circle facing each other. Half the circle consisted of Team A, the other half, of Team B. I would present a flash card that contained a word or phrase from a text we'd recently read. Then, alternating by team, one student would demonstrate it through pantomime. If the flash card read *cut*, for example, a student might act out using scissors. A correct action gained a point for the student's team.

The score was five to four. Team A was ahead by one. Soe Lin's turn was next. As the last person on Team B, he had a chance to tie up the game. The pressure was building. Team A members had already broken into applause. They knew Soe Lin's vocabulary was still weaker than anyone else's.

I held the flash card above my head. *Crossed arms*, it read.

"Soe Lin," I announced. "Cross your arms."

The room went from loud cheering to silence. Soe Lin's face lit up with his notorious smile—all dimples and teeth. His eyes darted around the circle as he searched for a cheater to discreetly show him the action. No one came to his rescue. I waited, hoping as usual, giving him extra time.

Just when I turned away to declare a win for the opposing team, in my peripheral vision I saw Soe Lin tentatively fold his arms across his chest. He glanced at me as if to say, "Is this it?" Then he quickly dropped his arms onto his lap.

"He did it! He did it!" I yelled, the only one to witness Soe Lin's fleeting gesture. Miguel Ángel and Gustavo from the other team refused to believe me. They both leapt from their chairs and jumped up and down hollering, "No, he didn't. No, he didn't."

"Soe Lin went like this," I argued, imitating what he'd done. "And that *is* crossing your arms."

Soe Lin leaned back in his seat, legs stretched out in front of him, arms now conveniently crossed. Based on his grin, he liked being the subject of the discussion. He looked from Miguel Ángel to Gustavo to me a few times, his head moving like the ball in a pinball machine.

As the heated debate died down, Soe Lin finally came to his own defense. He leaned forward, punched his chest hard with both fists, and shouted, "Tol' you, nigga!"

Another silence, this time of disbelief, maybe even shock. Then raucous laughter. At that moment Soe Lin officially joined the ranks of being cool. His singular action had revealed to his classmates—and to me—that he too cared about maintaining an acceptable self-image.

As a teacher, I realized he'd been tuned in since his first step into my portable, albeit to his peers. He'd heard plenty of kids say, "Tol' you, nigga." It was a phrase as commonplace in our predominantly nonwhite school as "What time is it?" He wasn't socialized enough yet to understand the offensive nature of the word *nigga*, but he understood the contextual appropriateness of what he'd said.

I considered using his response as a teachable moment, then decided against it. Doing so would have taken away from his breakthrough moment. Also, I questioned the fairness of chastising him for using the phrase since he'd witnessed others use it repeatedly with no repercussions. It would have been another instance of being singled out, and he'd already suffered a lot of those during his brief history in the United States. Besides, explaining the negative connotation of the epithet would have been more than his English proficiency could handle.

Over the years, colleagues commented on the sweet dispositions of my ESL students, seeming to insinuate they were more easily managed. Maybe also implying they were a different breed from the rest of the school population. My own perspective, gained from spending a lot more time with these kids and knowing them far beyond a superficial level, was that they were not any *sweeter*, but, yes, they were generally better behaved. This I contributed to three things. First, my students were new to the school environment. Second, teachers in their countries of origin were more likely to be revered, even feared. Third, negative self-expression among young people in their countries wasn't as tolerated.

However, in their need to be part of the culture, to be accepted, my students were no different from their American-born counterparts. And so eventually, inevitably, they assumed attitudes of dismissiveness, disrespect, belligerence. Yet, surprisingly, despite the language barrier and social obstacles—and, in Soe Lin's case, his diminutive size—they found a way to fit in while mostly steering clear of conflict. They had an admirable resilience, it seemed to me.

Soe Lin's reputation and behavior shifted dramatically that day of his victory. He stopped mumbling and trying to avoid others' attention. By the end of seventh grade, he displayed a temper, and he willingly defended himself by engaging in fistfights. He also had trouble containing his emotions and, on occasion, had to be restrained from hurting others. He paced, fumed, and swung at the air. He suffered disciplinary action. Fortunately, this phase of episodic flare-ups didn't last. Yet he did become rough around the edges, dyeing his hair orange and wearing his cap backwards. He bragged about gang members he'd met or known in Houston—but that was the extent of it. Just talk.

In the end, Soe Lin hardened but remained a decent kid, eager to learn. He represented an outcome that teachers hope for all students. He learned enough English to converse with anyone and make friends. By eighth grade he constantly chatted during class, incorporating the "vernacular" of his peers. He even volunteered to participate. "This is easy, dude," he'd exclaim as he marched to the front of the room to recite a short poem, spell a word on the board, or rearrange a sentence.

"Oh, Soe Lin," somebody would tease. "You think you so great." His classmates seemed irritated and impressed at the same time.

"I am," he kidded back, laughing. He often insisted on reading out loud, and when other students did it he'd point out their errors. Yet his goofy personality rarely offended.

My favorite Soe Lin memory is of hearing him glide on his skateboard along the cement walls and ramps surrounding the portable. I could tell when he arrived and when he was going home. I knew when he was practicing or showing off by the sounds of gravelly stops and bumps as he leapt from one ledge to a lower one. I'd hear girls shout, "Stop, Soe Lin," annoyed as they moved aside to avoid a collision.

Soe Lin inherited the skateboard from my son. Once Jonas had outgrown it, I'd brought it to school. I intended to keep it locked up in the portable and let any student borrow it. Instead, Soe Lin created a designated cubby for *his* skateboard.

"Ah, Miss, where you get that?" he demanded when he first happened to notice the shiny red cruiser on one of the closet shelves at the back of the room.

"Oh, that. It used to be my son's, but he doesn't want it anymore," I explained.

"Can I have it, Miss? Please?" he asked, breaking into his celebrated grin.

"How about if you borrow it for a day? Then other people can use it too," I suggested.

He nodded. "Okay."

That afternoon, seconds after the dismissal bell, Soe Lin appeared in my doorway. "Miss, can I take home today?" he asked.

"What are you talking about?" I asked. Our initial exchange about the skateboard had transpired eight hours earlier.

He walked toward the closet. "The red skate," he replied, baffled at my confusion. He'd even memorized which door out of the row of six nondescript ones to open.

He reached in and grabbed the "skate." Cradling it, he said, "This one. You remember now?"

"Okay. But just for tonight. I want you to put it back here before school tomorrow." I rested my hand where I wanted the skateboard returned.

"Yeah, just tonight. No problem," he assured me. "Thank you, Miss," he yelled as he headed out the door. I vowed to get him a helmet.

A radiant Soe Lin arrived the next morning, "skate" in tow, and placed it where I'd instructed. But he took it home that evening and every evening after. He and the skateboard became inseparable except during school hours. We never discussed him taking possession of it. Frankly, I couldn't have refused him if he'd asked. The skateboard symbolized a final step in aspiring to become a full-fledged American teenager.

None of the other students ever asked about the skateboard. I suspected they were secretly happy for Soe Lin for finding a passion. His newfound mode of transportation brought me joy as well. To see him sail along on that "skate" made me imagine he might sail along his path in life as freely. After all, he deserved a few lucky breaks.

Too Young, Too Old

We sat in the empty classroom, at a corner of the spacious work area composed of four standard rectangular tables lined up. We weren't working but eating, our lunches spread before us. Irene had deliberately angled her bag of chips to have easy access. I'd done the same with my carrots and hummus.

"Do you want an egg, Irene?" I asked, saying my student's name as close to the Spanish pronunciation as I could: *ee-RAY-nay*, so much prettier than its English equivalent. I loved rolling the name off my tongue and did so every chance I got. I uncovered a glass dish containing the two hard-boiled eggs. Irene studied them, chose the smaller one, and carefully placed it on her Styrofoam cafeteria plate.

"Protein is very important for us right now," I advised. Irene nodded in serious agreement, her big eyes unblinking. Both pregnant for the first time, she at fourteen and I at forty, we were sharing a meal, talking about food and our health habits, our fears and joys. An unusual student-teacher bond had formed between us, despite the cultural and language barriers, despite the age barrier. Or maybe the bond was *because* of how old we were: each of us, being at opposite ends of the "age of pregnancy" spectrum, challenged mainstream opinion.

Personally, I felt a bit uncomfortable about Irene's pregnancy. As her teacher, I couldn't condone it. But it was her persona that proved the equalizer in our relationship. Despite her youth, she embodied maturity. She was a stoic female leader among the students, always available for counsel. They nicknamed her Mamacita, and she became everyone's mother. Large in stature and presence, she let nothing fluster her. Whether in the middle of a dance party, during a passionate yelling match, or while offering words of encouragement, she spoke in the same even tone. And since her face rarely revealed emotion, she emanated a certain calm.

For instance, one morning I witnessed Irene right in the face of a distraught, slightly younger girl named Fabiola. "Why you crying for *that*?" Irene demanded. *That* was a spiraling conflict sparked by an anonymous note found on the floor of the girls' restroom. "You don' know. Maybe your friends don' tell the truth 'bout you." Irene had reduced the fight to what it was—hearsay—and it instantly became a forgivable misunderstanding. Fabiola wiped lingering tears on the back of a lace sleeve and nodded in concession.

Over many lunches, Irene and I had spoken freely of our pregnancy milestones. Morning sickness. The switch to maternity clothes. The delightful surprise of feeling the baby kick. We listened to each other and tried to withhold judgment. Gratitude dominated my journey. Although aware of the physical risks of having a first baby at forty, I'd still waited until the eleventh hour; and yet, at least up to that point, I was experiencing a healthy pregnancy. At the same time I, in my cultural bubble, assumed that gratitude wasn't the defining emotion for Irene's pregnancy. *Fourteen is too young to become a parent*, I thought. *At fourteen having a baby is an inconvenience.*

Flip a coin, though, and in Irene's world forty was too old. I wondered if she felt sorry for me, destined to have only one baby in my lifetime. Just the week before, she'd introduced her mother to me. A young but weary face had peered from the driver's window of a minivan. Kids filled the vehicle from front to back to way back. Waving to Irene and her family as they drove off, I realized I couldn't possibly serve as a role model for her. I didn't compete with her mother's cascading pregnancies.

Now, Irene took more chips from the bag and said, "When my mom have fourteen years like me, she have two babies." She held up two fingers. "In Mexico, everybody love babies. They want many babies."

"Really?" Chewing on an apple, I weighed the value of economic security and life manageability against large, gregarious, fun-loving families that spanned generations. "And how many children does your mom have now?"

"Eight. But one die. My grandma have eleven sons. All in Mexico. In Veracruz."

I did nothing remarkable as far as changing the course of events in Irene's life. But I do believe our lunches and our relationship benefited her. Although not a mentor in a strict sense, I tried to impart to her the importance of health during pregnancy—and maybe even a slight sense of awe at the approaching miracle of giving birth, since I myself was certainly feeling awestruck.

Who knows to what extent I helped her? In any case, circumstances had allowed us a genuine connection. Such a thing didn't happen very often, nor was it to be taken for granted. Teens appreciate, and probably have always appreciated, adults who listen but refrain from lecturing. I was able to be such a person for Irene at a critical time.

Throughout my career teaching ESL, principals and teachers commented on the strong bonds I formed with my students, and on how detailed my comments were on written assessments. One day I decided to push the issue. When an administrator remarked on my skill personalizing student evaluations, I pressed her. "Well, thanks. But why do you think I'm able to do that?" After a few seconds of silence, I answered my own question. "I have forty-two kids on my roll, while most teachers have one hundred and fifty."

"I know," my administrator said with a sigh, as she adjusted her walkie-talkie to temper the voices booming from it, demanding her immediate presence elsewhere. "Tell me about it." She waved goodbye as she hurried down the hall. She'd avoided the contentious issue of class size. It did seem like a waste of breath, even way back then.

For some fortunate reason involving complex government funding issues, my job description restricted me to teaching only immigrant students—that is, those who had resided in the United States for no more than three years. Because of the number of pupils enrolled with that qualifier, some semesters my total class load was forty to fifty students. By comparison, a typical secondary teacher taught around three times that many, year after year. My situation exemplified the advantages of a smaller teacher-student ratio. Simply put, I gave Irene time and attention and formed a relationship with her because I had fewer students to contend with.

My experience of working with smaller groups of students validated my belief that teachers provide an invaluable resource in education. A more valuable resource, I'd venture to say, than technology, books, furniture, sports facilities and coaches, secretaries, or administrators. Studies have shown that quality teaching is the number-one determining factor linked to student achievement. I credit my successes to the manageability of the relatively small number of students in my charge.

Although Irene and I divulged much about our pregnancies to each other, I never inquired about the identity of her baby's father. Somehow the subject felt irrelevant. Nor did she seem compelled to share it. The idea of the father being a middle-schooler struck me as unlikely. The male students, like the females, treated Irene with reverence, behaving more like her children than her peers. None of the boys dared to demean her, or even flirt with her. She had an inner beauty as well as an outer one—flawless skin, perfectly round cheeks, silky waist-length hair—and both contributed to her esteemed position.

In late April, preparations for the Cinco de Mayo program were underway. Irene, fiercely proud of her Mexican heritage, was invested in its success. Male-female partners arranged themselves on the auditorium stage to practice a traditional dance that Irene had insisted on including in the program. The folk dance hailed from Veracruz, her birthplace. On this day, two of the male positions stood vacant. No surprise. These boys were the weak link. They'd agreed to participate the day before, but only after a series of pleas and fervent prodding from the girls. It now seemed their capitulation had been temporary.

Yet the dance couldn't happen without them. None of the six pairs was optional. Irene dropped her dance partner's hand and walked to the edge of the stage, shielding her eyes from the bright theater lights. "Oscar, Sergio, where you are?" she asked in a firm voice.

No response. Just the pitter-patter of feet scampering for a place to hide in the balcony. I'd reserved the auditorium for the class period. Students not needed on the stage entertained themselves exploring all the nooks and crannies of a space rarely accessible to them.

"I hear you. But we don' see you," she announced. "Don' be babies. Yesterday you dance. And today, no?" Silence from the ranks. She turned and pointed to the waiting dancers. Muffled giggles floated from the upper rows of the ground floor to Irene. Standing with hands on hips, staring into the darkness, she called out, "We counting on you. Yesterday you promise. Now you break it. That's not right.

Come down. Don' be chickens. I can teach you."

Gradually the performers settled their bony arms and legs on the stage floor at various angles. They started chatting and forgot about Oscar and Sergio. Irene sat down at the edge of the stage, quiet, her legs dangling. I knew, though, that she hadn't given up.

Like toddlers who stop their misconduct only after the attention they're getting is withdrawn, the two boys sheepishly appeared from behind the folds of the giant curtain. Irene slid playfully back to her center-stage position, sashaying like a ballerina. Nobody reacted negatively to her playfulness. They were forever willing to give her the benefit of the doubt. She was the leader. I imagined that her own children would treat her with the same respect and reverence.

My son was born in April of Irene's eighth-grade year. I took maternity leave for the remainder of the spring semester. Irene's baby was due sometime that summer.

The following school year one of her friends filled me in on Irene's situation: she was attending high school, and she'd had a baby boy like me.

"Don' worry, Miss," Irene had assured me during one of our lunches in my classroom. "I'm not stop school. When I'm go to school, my mom is with my baby."

Perhaps having a baby flowed with the natural progression of her life. I trusted her instincts, having seen them in action many times.

Lessons from ESL Bees

It was showtime. Chaos spread across the room. The kids had waited for this moment since class began, more than an hour earlier, when I'd promised them a movie. Now, in a matter of minutes, they managed to push away all the tables and slide their chairs haphazardly before the big white pull-down screen. They kept their backpacks at their feet to sneak chips and sips of soda while they watched the film. I pretended not to notice. During the hustle, someone had lowered the blinds. But since it was almost noon and springtime in Texas, sunlight streamed through the bent plastic slats, giving the portable a soft glow.

Each May I showed *Spellbound* to my students. The documentary followed fourteen middle-school spelling bee finalists from across the country through their personal journeys to the national competition in Washington, D.C. I'd stumbled upon it a few years earlier, and when it hit me that a third of the finalists were immigrant students, I became inspired to create a watered-down version of a spelling bee in my school.

Spellbound offered great role models for my students, especially the first finalist presented. Angela was from West Texas. The film spent a fair amount of time introducing her two parents. Neither one spoke English, and both had illegally crossed the Mexican border into Texas. The camera zoomed in on her father, a cattle herder on a ranch. He stood on a fence rung and whistled, his eyes on a vast horizon with cliffs in the distance, sheepishly avoiding the camera. Her mother was filmed crocheting as she listened to TV news. My students from Mexico undoubtedly could relate. Then the scene switched to a pep rally being held in Angela's honor in her school gymnasium, shortly before she was to travel to D.C. Cheerleaders performed in front of a blue curtain to a rowdy crowd. Angela was presented with a teddy bear twice her size. My students were impressed that so much attention was being given to a single student—especially one whose parents didn't speak English.

Next, the pimply, white face of a nerdy-looking boy filled the screen. *"Ew!"* my students squealed in disgust, with some turning their heads away. The boy scrunched up his brow, bit his lip, and stared directly into the camera. It zoomed in even closer to capture him gazing at the ceiling for several agonizing seconds, desperately trying to retrieve information from somewhere deep in his brain. Finally, he faced the camera with a wide grin, revealing two gleaming rows of braces.

"¡Muy feo!" Leticia had found the nerdy boy very unattractive.

Quick to pass judgment, my students didn't yet understand what was happening.

"Miss, this ugly movie," complained Juan." Let's see *Fast and Furious*. That's cool movie."

"Listen! That boy is participating in a competition," I explained. "We're going to have one too. And, just like in the movie, your friends and families can come watch."

Slowly, the kids became engrossed, as I knew they would, and a hush fell over the classroom. Some students perched on the edge of seats. Others sat on hands, glued to the screen. A few squirmed when a participant misspelled a word and walked off the stage in tears.

At one point a contestant dressed in her plaid school uniform struggled at the microphone with a word she was unsure of. Everyone watching—parents, the panel of judges, the news teams—hung onto each letter that rolled off her tongue. No longer able to hold back a flood of tears, the girl closed her eyes and began to move her lips in prayer. It was nerve-racking as she slowly pronounced a few more letters, then changed her mind, paused, and started again. I glanced at Lupe, my student always open to the dramatic. Her head was bent over on the top of her backpack, usually carried in front of her, and she covered her eyes. Her hands trembled with the anxiety of witnessing this girl fail in front of so many official-looking people. When the contestant was applauded for a correct response and returned to her seat on stage, Lupe dropped the backpack to the floor and hooted in relief. The camera quickly panned to the girl's mother in the audience, holding her fist high in the air and beaming. My students now understood that a spelling bee presented a great opportunity to make family members proud.

"We're gonna play this game?" Marta, my strongest student, asked. By the look on her face, I could tell she already relished the idea of victory. Without pausing for my answer she proclaimed, "Yeah, this gonna be tight!"

An annual spelling bee solely for ESL students offered a solution to a variety of issues. The University Interscholastic League (UIL), created by The University of Texas at Austin over a century ago, sponsors an annual series of statewide contests. Students can compete in a slew of academic and elective subjects, from band to mathematics to debate. Yet UIL generally isn't on immigrant students' radars. Their level of English proficiency precludes them from being competitive, except in art or athletics or music. And even then, there's the problem of catching up. Take band or orchestra as an example. By the end of fifth grade, most students, at least in Texas, have to choose electives—subjects like band, orchestra, choir, and theater—for their middle-school years. If they select band or orchestra, they have to decide on an instrument as well. Immigrant students don't necessarily enter an American public school by fifth grade; so, in many cases, band or orchestra is a missed opportunity for them. After years of watching my students be on the sideline for extracurricular activities like UIL, I'd decided to create a competition exclusively for them.

The spelling bee also provided a culminating year-end activity. A firm believer in teaching phonemes (the smallest unit of sound when pronouncing a word), I began my daily lessons with a fifteen-minute focus on the *b* sound, or the *th* sound, or any of the other forty-two phonemes in the English language. I also believed strongly in teaching spelling patterns (Remember "*i* before *e* except after *c*"?), and by May my students were comfortably familiar with them. The bee was a fitting way for them to demonstrate what they'd learned during the year. In addition, it gave the kids an opportunity to employ oral comprehension, vocabulary, and presentation skills, as well as to build their overall confidence. Besides, with the end of a tedious school year on the horizon, that last month required a major shift in routine to keep students engaged.

When I first came up with the idea of a spelling bee, my challenge was to devise an experience that all students would eagerly participate in. The event needed to be somewhat formal and challenging, yet one in which all of them could have some degree of success. To compensate for their limited language, I gave them the official spelling list weeks ahead of time so they might study and prepare on their own.

I also devoted class time to practice. The most popular activity for reviewing spelling words was the game known as "hangman." All I had to do was point to the large right-angle figure drawn on the whiteboard and five or six students would dash to play. After short blanks were added below the figure, students shouted out letters to guess at the word in question.

One area of activity, called a "center" in classroom jargon, was a table covered with Scrabble tiles placed face-up. Since this game was less action-packed, students could take their time during practice. Lupe and Rafael always jumped at the chance to work with the wooden letter tiles. She'd stare at them as he read a specific word from his spelling list, which he had difficulty keeping flat since it stayed rolled up to easily fit in his pants pocket or the top section of his backpack.

"*Lady*," Rafael said.

"*Lady?*" Lupe repeated.

Rafael nodded.

"You mean, like women?" Lupe snarled at him. They had a contentious friendship, in part due to her stubborn nature, that was always interesting to observe.

Rafael shrugged. He wasn't supposed to give clues. Lupe slapped her palm on the table. "I hate you, Rafael," she yelled. But an *L* tile could already be seen between two of her fingers, all of which ended in fake curled nails painted blue.

The next center was a table stacked with mini-chalkboards, erasers, and plenty of chalk. A member of the group working there would read aloud a word. Whoever first spelled it correctly on their chalkboard received a point. Winners were rewarded with extra credit.

A table in another center was set up for those few brave students who went for the utmost challenge: creating crosswords with Scrabble tiles. For the worksheet lovers or those students who preferred working alone, I provided fill-in-the-blank pages. One letter would be missing from each word, and students would try to complete the list of thirty words by resorting to their spelling lists. As for my dyslexic students, they avoided the competitive activities altogether. Instead, they dictated words to each other at the computer station.

After several days of spending time at the centers, we moved on to simulation spelling bees in small groups. Eventually we practiced together as a whole class. I added various props, with the table bell usually coming first. I'd tap the bell when students misspelled a word to signal they had to leave the circle of participants.

Introducing the microphone came last, always during one of the final dress rehearsals before the actual bee—and it changed everything. Some students felt repulsed, as if the object were a dangerous, slithering snake. While they seemed drawn to the microphone's novelty and official appeal, it terrified them. They winced hearing their voices projected across the room, then froze and went silent. But a few, including theatrical Marta, loved speaking and singing into it. For them, the microphone was ultimate proof that, just like the kids in *Spellbound*, they were truly going to perform.

Throughout all the preparation for the spelling bee, and during it too, something frustrated me: my students' resistance to using one important strategy to their benefit. An official spelling bee rule states that if a contestant requests a sentence containing the word to be spelled, the announcer is required to provide one—in fact, to provide as many sentences as are requested. For an ESL learner, sentences are key in clarifying words in the English lexicon. Hearing a word in isolation, without a frame of reference, without context, requires skill in distinguishing sounds. That's tough when English isn't someone's first language. For example, Spanish speakers struggle with the slight sound variation between the short vowel sounds of *i* and *e*. They easily mistake *bill* for *bell*, and *sit* for *set*. The same is true with the vowel sounds in *slip* and *sleep*, and *hit* and *heat*. Such pairs of words are called minimal pairs, meaning that they differ in only one sound. And that difference may be barely audible to people learning English.

I did everything in my power to encourage students

to pose this question: "Can I have a sentence, please?" I explained its importance numerous times. We recited it over and over. They wrote it down as a dictation exercise. Later, I posted it in extra-large letters on the wall. I jumped up and down whenever kids asked the question of their own volition during a practice bee. A few of my students caught on and consistently requested sentences. But, to my disappointment, the majority continued to resist. Instead, they guessed at the spelling words—and often misspelled them.

At last, the much anticipated and dreaded day arrived. As always, it made me happy to see that most students had heeded my advice and came dressed in formal attire. The boys wore freshly ironed slacks and collared shirts, while the girls had on lacy spring-colored dresses and high-heeled shoes. Most of them got there before the first bell in hopes of finding out who the unlucky contestants were—that is, the first five or so to march to the microphone. Since no one ever volunteered to go first, I had to determine the sequence of competitors by randomly drawing names from a box. I did this alone in the portable, on the eve of the bee.

Ideally, the first contestant would be a strong speller—it upped the chances for the bee to have a smooth beginning. I was adamant, though, about maintaining the random selection process, since it allowed my students a real-life experience, one in which they weren't safeguarded from failure. Yet no matter who ended up going first, my heart went out to that student.

"Ms. Smith, you can please tell us who have to go first? Please, we wanna know," begged Liliana, the spokesperson for the tense crowd.

"I don' care if you pick me first. I'm not go first," argued Miguel Ángel, who was particularly belligerent in the morning.

To calm nerves, I quickly read the list of names in

order of participation. As I did so, a few students fled out the door, slamming it behind them, in search of the ones at the top of the list. They relished being the bearer of bad news. Others put their heads down on the table, finally able to relax in the knowledge that they'd lucked out in this lotto.

Once the bell for first period sounded, students knew to report to the library. I busied myself with final preparations, displaying the first-, second-, and third-place trophies at the judge's table, along with their matching gift certificates. I placed thirty-four participation ribbons in neat rows. Magaly and Claudia immediately volunteered to direct students to their numbered seats. Trickling in, they surprisingly followed the two girls' zealous instructions and headed to their designated spots. Waiting in the chairs were the "number necklaces" I'd made for each student: a paper attached to a string with an identifying number written on it. Following my instructions, they slung their numbers over their heads.

I busied myself arranging parent refreshments on paper plates, all the while wishing some miracle of physics would erase the remaining fifteen minutes before showtime. (It never bodes well when middle-schoolers are unoccupied.) But time marched forward as usual, and with each minute my students found new ways to stave off boredom. Miguel Ángel and Eligio started wrestling, seated, from the waist up. Camila, Yasmín, and a few others exchanged seats, grinning, thinking they were pulling something over on me. Heriberto and José Luis darted to the door to yell at buddies passing by. Then several boys moved into stage two: transforming their numbers into paper airplanes they sailed through the air at various angles and heights. Trying my best to ignore all of them—*they're releasing stress*, I told myself—I took attendance and checked the microphone one last time.

At the height of the commotion, in walked Mr. Infante, judge for the spelling bee. Young, Spanish-speaking, and the after-school soccer coach, he was a highly popular teacher, and the students hooted and joked with him: "Hey, Elefante. What you doing here, dude?"

But Mr. Infante stared straight ahead and acknowledged no one as he took his chair at the table facing the contestants. I appreciated his determination to stay neutral and maintain a degree of propriety.

Excitement bubbled over as families and friends drifted in. Not only was the audience growing; the number of onlookers was too. Kids on their way to class stalled by the library windows, waving, mock gang-signing to look cool, before the hall monitors hastened them to their destinations. My students felt, for once, that they were the center of attention. Today was their day.

By now, the anxiety was visible all around. The younger girls fanned themselves with their numbers like elderly church women. One or two looked like they might faint. Faces glistened with sweat. Eyes blinked double-time. Final bathroom trips were taken, leaving the rows checkered with empty chairs.

"Miss, Sandra throw up in the restroom!" Claudia reported to me, panic-stricken. Before I had a chance to respond, Mr. Alonso, the assistant principal, strode into the library dressed in a fashionable gray suit and tie. He wore a carnation in his breast pocket for this most special of ceremonies. I felt moved by the gesture of support. He took the microphone in hand but said nothing as he waited for the audience and participants to settle down. As usual, this took a few excruciating minutes. Yet he continued to wait, unflustered.

Finally, Mr. Alonso led the Pledge of Allegiance then gave a warm welcome. He spoke mostly in Spanish, translating parts of his speech into English for the few parents from Iraq and Congo. As he talked, I skimmed the small group of family members in attendance, trying not to feel disappointed at the low turnout. Half of a lesson had been spent making elaborate hand-drawn invitations for students

49

to take home. Closer to the event, the school's parent liaison had made a follow-up phone call to each child's household. The bee offered parents a rare opportunity to see their children perform on an individual basis. But I reminded myself that many parents held two jobs, and that some had night jobs and slept during the day.

As Master of Ceremonies, I introduced the thirty-four participants, including the apparently recovered Sandra, who had slipped back into the library. One by one, students stood as I announced their name, country of origin, and length of time in the United States. It was important for the audience to understand that students in this country for three months were at a disadvantage over those who had been here for, say, two years. My heart warmed as a few fathers sitting in the back, arms folded across their middle, nodded in appreciation, and maybe resignation, of this reality—that most things involved an unequal playing field. Mothers seemed to know they were at the event to support all students, not just their own; and in between reaching for an overly active toddler, they clapped, their eyes half-closed, as each student stood.

We were ready for the first contestant. I watched Lupe approach the stand. She wore a dress instead of the usual jeans, tank top, and oversized sweatshirt. With the dress, plus her curly brown hair neatly brushed to one side and adorned with a glittery gold barrette, she could have been attending her first communion. An eighth-grader possessing an energy that encouraged people to seek out her friendship and approval, she was a leader among her peers. Although no shining star in spelling, she did make a suitable first contestant.

Lupe had been my student for seventh grade too. Watching her now as she took her time positioning the microphone, I realized how familiar I was, after two years, with her history, her learning style, her strengths and weaknesses, gifts and flaws.

Among the many reasons I enjoyed Lupe was her unpredictability. She was a union of opposites. One situation she would embrace with absolute courage, while another would cause her to shut down for fear of failure. Once, during a summer camp held at my house, she was the first to jump into an inner tube in the middle of a deep, cold lake. Having only swum in a city pool before that afternoon, she'd agreed to have a motorboat pull her at full speed for nearly a mile with only a life preserver to protect her. She shrieked in utter joy and terror the entire ride. And yet when asked to read out loud in front of the class, she would put her head on the table and cover her ears. Her perfectionism had gotten in the way.

I often thought Lupe's confidence level was mood-dependent. And her mood was linked to what kind of night she'd had at home. One morning, still dark outside, she walked into my portable sooner than the other early birds. I was at my computer writing. She sat down at the table nearest me with her backpack attached to her front. She seemed almost despondent, and I assumed that she simply needed some quiet time.

"I hate my mother," Lupe blurted out, her broken voice interrupting the silence. Then she confided that she'd had to sleep on the kitchen floor because her mother's boyfriend spent the night. Her feeling of abandonment saturated the room like a heavy fog.

"I want go back to Mexico. Live with my grandma. She my real mom. I miss my grandma too much." She cried, wiping away huge teardrops with a sleeve.

"I know your mother loves you," I said to console her.

"No, she not," Lupe argued, quickly turning her head to hide the tears. Understandably, she was yearning for her grandmother, who had raised her until two years ago, and for her small community in Mexico, so provincial and different from her apartment-dwelling life here.

Now, I returned my focus to the spelling bee and to Lupe. I looked for signs indicating her mood this morning. She appeared calm and ready. I pronounced the word she would need to spell. "*Dig.*" I enunciated it with extreme care.

Lupe knew this word. There was absolutely no doubt in my mind. It topped the list the class had reviewed for weeks. And we'd just finished reading the novel *Holes* and watching the movie based on it. In both, boys assigned to a boot camp had to *dig* holes all day long.

Yet Lupe's face went blank. She asked me to repeat the word. I did so numerous times. I considered what she was finding problematic about the word *dig*. Maybe it was the final consonant sound. To her ears, maybe the *guh* sound appeared to be a *cuh* sound. I felt panic set in. Did Lupe think I was saying *dick*?

Her uncertainty about the word baffled me, and I began to doubt myself. Had students not bothered to study because I'd made the list too accessible? Furthermore, Lupe refused to do the one simple thing that could help her: ask for a sentence with the word *dig* in it. Was she choosing today, of all days, to resort to stubbornness? Or was she intimidated by the adults in the audience and ashamed to ask for assistance?

She shifted the microphone from one hand to the other. She repeated the word in an affirmative tone as if coaching herself. It was hard to tell whether she was saying *dick* or *dig*.

Then she again switched to a question. "*Dig?*" Her eyes pleaded with me.

I beamed this to her: *Say, "Can I have a sentence, please?" Then I can answer, "The boys dig holes in the hot sun."*

In the next instant, realizing Lupe had no intention of using the primary tool at her disposal, I surrendered my role as teacher and became solely the pronouncer of words. I nodded my head, sat back, and folded my arms, done with her shenanigans.

But Lupe wasn't ready to give up. She scanned the audience imploringly, like a lost child at a carnival. She shifted her weight from one foot to the other and let the microphone fall to her side. Finally, a wave of determination prevailed, and taking a deep breath into the microphone, she began. *"D - I -* [long pause] *- C - K,"* she slowly spelled.

My hand slid the few inches to the table bell. I lightly tapped it. Lupe glared at me in utter disbelief.

The audience's reaction was surprisingly reserved, all except Miguel Ángel's and Heriberto's. These two were renowned for their knowledge of English slang and profanity. Miguel Ángel immediately yelled out in his thick Cuban accent, "Oh my God! She spell *dick* and she don' even know what she did. Ha ha ha!"

Thankfully, none of the other students joined in since they had no clue about the significance of Lupe's mistake. But this year's spelling bee, over all, hadn't gotten off to a good start, and I worked quickly to resurrect it before Miguel Ángel and Heriberto got even more out of hand. I motioned for contestant number two to come forward as Lupe angrily huffed to her seat in the audience. She disappeared among the supportive arms of her female fan club—both immigrant and Chicana.

Despite the rocky opening, the spelling bee turned out well. Amazingly, the competition went on for sixty-three rounds. (In previous years we'd been lucky to reach round twenty.) It lasted a solid fifty minutes, and Lupe's best friend, Sylvie, won a trophy by taking second place. That brought Lupe's anger toward me down a notch or two. Sylvie glowed with happiness, as did Lupe.

At the much later date of writing this, I now see that Lupe had led me specifically to have a greater appreciation for courage—and to differentiate between courage and boldness. I'd always considered Lupe bold, but her courage involved more vulnerability. She was the kind of learner who felt she must be perfect every step of the way. The day of the spelling bee, when she went first, she was clearly not perfect. And this had been evident in front of many people, mostly strangers. Yet she'd charged through, keeping her fears in check.

I thought back to my adolescence. I wondered if there had ever been a time when I demonstrated courage the way Lupe had during that bee. I remembered feeling terrified of being shamed or humiliated in front of others. I avoided situations that could bring me embarrassment. For instance, I didn't participate in talent shows. Nor did I talk to boys I secretly liked in case the feelings weren't mutual. I wanted guarantees. Yet here I was, many years later, expecting qualities from my students that I myself hadn't possessed at their age.

In the weeks after the bee, I started to appreciate how brave all my students had to be every day of their lives. They feared getting lost, being called names, or having their belongings stolen by other students. They were targeted by bullies who took advantage of their naiveté, of not knowing systems or protocols or the language. When they were bullied in P.E. or any other class, they couldn't easily explain what had happened, so they kept quiet about the mistreatment. They avoided speaking directly to the kids involved or to the proper authorities. There seemed to be no recourse but to suffer the cruelties of their peers.

My students spent the school day trying to conceal their accent, pronunciation, and broken English. They lived in terror of being called on in front of an entire class, being snickered at because of their English or their clothing or their different smell or appearance. It was one thing for a nonimmigrant student to fail in front of an audience in middle school, but an immigrant student who failed suffered an added layer of shame.

During my teaching career, throughout any given year I got asked the same type of question by students numerous times: "Ms. Smith, you can change my schedule, please? I don't like my class of science [or whatever subject]."

"Why?" I'd probe.

"Because I'm alone."

"Alone?" I feigned surprise. "You mean it's only you and the teacher?" I teased, knowing full well what they meant: nobody else from ESL was in that specific class. No other students shared their struggle with a new language. "It's okay," I assured them. "You'll learn more English that way."

I often felt a twinge of guilt for having glossed over their feeling of isolation. Easy for me to say it was good for them. I'd never had to sit for forty-five or ninety minutes a day in a classroom of thirty people who spoke another language. How much worse it would be if there was no one around I was comfortable with to help me understand. That *would* be a scary place. Did I really think they learned better or faster? Some did, but more of them were apt to shut down.

What's more, some of my students suffered from post-traumatic stress. In going to the United States from their native countries, they'd had to leave behind extended family members central to their childhood. Many had suffered long, arduous, and dangerous journeys, forced to trust strangers in the process. Not ever wanting to pry, I rarely asked my Spanish-speaking students how they'd come to live in Texas. Yet pieces of information occasionally surfaced in everyday conversations.

Once, on a hike through woods along a dry creek bed, a few students shared how the landscape reminded them of their journey to Texas and the many days of walking through thickets of trees. They talked about hiding when the sun was out and trekking for miles in the dark. Of going days without food or water.

Another time the class read a novel together in which the main character's sibling dies. My student Fernando, a slight and soft-spoken sixth-grader, suddenly shared a personal story. He described his older brother drowning right beside him as they swam across the Rio Grande into Texas. "We crossing. The water start coming real fast. And coming like this." He held a thin arm above his head to show how high the water reached. "I do this." With his hand out, he demonstrated trying to catch his brother, who was beyond his grasp. He shook his head. "He go down in the water. I don' see him no more."

Fernando was barely audible, but the class heard every word. A respectful silence followed.

"Was it just you and your brother? Or were other people there at the river?" I eventually asked.

"Just me and my brother." He shook his head again. "We have a coyote just for a little. Before. In Mexico. But not at the fast water." Coyotes charged immigrants an inordinate amount of money to smuggle them out of one country and into another.

One year my student Marta, also from Mexico, spent every lunch period eating in the portable with me. During class, Marta was meticulous and well prepared, always with two freshly sharpened pencils. She insisted on a front-row seat, which would afford good visibility. She was relentless in her need to understand exceptions to every grammatical rule. Nothing escaped her attention. In the span of two years, Marta progressed from a score of zero in all four language domains—speaking, listening, reading, writing—to a four or a five in each. A score of four is advanced, and a five is basically native-speaker proficiency.

One day over sandwiches, I offhandedly approached the subject of how she'd come to Texas. I thought somehow that her fastidiousness would translate into her having had the correct paperwork to legally enter the United States. I assumed Marta's story would be a tame one. But not so.

Marta recounted in detail how she and her mother traveled with a group under the guidance of a coyote. At some point they hid in a house. They slept on the floor and in closets. The house must have been located near the border. She didn't know. Nor did she know exactly how many days she spent hiding.

Then Marta got to the most frightening part: she and all the others had to flee without warning, guns firing at them as they ran for a waiting truck. "We're sleeping on the floor," she told me. "Is night and then the mens come and tell us, 'Everybody out! Hurry! Run! Run to the truck!' The shooting is loud. We go fast."

Some people were forced to run into the bush, Marta related. Yet she and her mother made it to the vehicle and were transported across the border.

After hearing Marta's story, I was even more amazed that she and my other students could function in school as well as they did. In Marta's case, though, I felt that at least in the United States she had everything it took to be happy and to achieve success in life: not only a supportive family, but also confidence, resourcefulness, perseverance, intelligence, and a hard shell.

In her eighth-grade year Marta enrolled in the humanities and fine arts magnet program at our school. It was a tremendous feat for a second language learner who had been in the United States only three years. Her progress was unprecedented. Yet as impressive as this was, she carried remnants of her painful past.

Once Marta had "graduated" from my classroom and the ESL program, she cut off interaction with me and her first set of friends. She'd been utterly attached to me for two years, sitting at my side during lunch and inhaling my every word. Later, she didn't even acknowledge me in the hallways. Nor did she stop by to chat. If I entered a classroom where she was present, she refused to meet my gaze. A separation from her country that involved gunfire was an explosive, definitive, and final way to separate. Maybe she'd learned to detach from everything in a similar way, no matter the circumstances. Run and don't look back.

At any rate, Marta's separation from me as her English teacher in Texas was extreme. I understood. I was a remnant of her past as an ESL student. She'd moved on. Now she spoke English fluently and was surrounded by an English-speaking population. Her new friends were athletes and journalists and leaders in student government. Her story had a happy ending. She became a bona fide American teenager. And I was glad for her achievements.

It was the first day back after summer vacation. The amazing sixty-three-round spelling bee the previous May seemed a distant memory. By mid-afternoon, returning students had let go of their shyness. Minutes before the dismissal bell, a few raised their hands.

"Hey, Miss. We gonna have the spelling bee like last year?" one piped up.

"That was so fun!" another one said.

"Yes, we will," I said. "But it's a long way off. It's at the end of the school year. In May." Remembering that many ESL students had trouble with the calendar, I clarified, "That is nine months from now."

Yet secretly I could hardly contain my happiness. My students had clearly not forgotten the spelling bee. In fact, it was foremost on their minds. They wanted to repeat it despite the challenges posed. I promised myself I'd be more empathetic as we prepared for it this year. I wouldn't discount, but instead acknowledge, my students' fears. I'd praise them for their courage, explaining that I recognized how hard it was to succeed. And how scary it was to fail.

But on that first day of school, I listened as a returning student declared, "I'm gonna win this time!"

A worthy goal, I thought. Then I beamed my shared enthusiasm with a smile.

Train Wreck

I noticed the white hand-embroidered tea towels wrapped in tissue paper once I sat down to begin class. The sisters must have carefully laid their gifts on top of my lesson-plan book when I was distracted. I slowly unwrapped the towels as my students looked on.

"The China girls make. For you," someone proclaimed, as proudly as if he, and not they, had given them to me.

"The *Chinese* girls," I corrected him. "The girls are *from* China."

To the two sisters I said, "Oh, how beautiful." My appreciation was genuine. White satin birds, flowers, and leaves had been delicately hand-stitched along the top borders of the cotton towels. Normally I disliked taking up class time with gift giving because it disrupted the flow of the lesson. I would feel torn—wanting to be polite and gracious to the gift bearers, yet wanting even more to set a serious academic tone at the beginning of class. Luckily, on that day and at that hour there were only ten students. I could take the time to appreciate the sisters' stunning craftsmanship without mayhem resulting.

"Did you sew them yourselves?" I asked, pantomiming pulling a threaded needle. They wouldn't have understood my question otherwise since they didn't speak English. Both girls responded with their customary gesture of cupping their hands over their mouths and laughing, which had led me to believe that showing teeth was frowned upon in China.

As I unfolded and laid the towels flat on a table for everyone to admire, I was struck by the quaintness of these handmade presents. The tiny stitchery required painstaking effort. I wondered how many hours it had taken the sisters to do this for me, and if they'd had any guidance. I pictured them sitting together and working the intricate patterns some days in the middle of a busy steamy kitchen, other days in front of a television that rambled on in a language they didn't understand. In the past, I'd received handmade cards from students and an occasional candle or box of chocolates at Christmas, but never anything so elaborate. I assured the girls that I loved them and would keep them forever. More blushing, giggling, and covering of their mouths. They seemed delighted that I was delighted.

I can easily recall the Chinese sisters' smiling faces. One was in sixth grade, the other in seventh. The only way to tell them apart was that the seventh-grader stood a fraction of an inch taller. She also appeared to be less shy, which is why people addressed her when they needed to communicate with the pair. I was simply glad they had each other.

They'd entered the school—its student body about 97 percent Black—speaking almost no English. And when they did try to speak their new language, it was incredibly hard to decipher. Much like two weeping willows in a forest of sky-reaching, solid oaks, the girls had a meekness that greatly contrasted with the boisterousness of the mainstream students. The school had a long-established reputation for being unruly, and the staff struggled to maintain control.

From the first day the sisters showed up in the front

office, an unspoken, low level of anxiety seemed to hover over the faculty—even over some of the students—as to whether the school was a good fit for them. Immigrant and refugee families often begin at the bottom of the economic ladder, living in poorer neighborhoods with challenged schools. The parents navigate blindly, lacking knowledge of the intricacies and reputations of local neighborhoods and public schools. And since they're simultaneously starting employment and establishing living arrangements in a new country, their children's school enrollment is rarely a top priority.

I myself shelved a cautionary inner voice that questioned the girls' safety, not wanting to acquiesce to the reality of a rough environment that lacked diversity. I chose to assume that after the newcomers had survived a few bumps in the road, school life would run smoothly for them.

The sisters sustained their good natures for a while. They smiled constantly, except when concentrating. Then their eyebrows would furrow in the shape of V's as they bent low to their papers or books.

Yet their extreme attachment to each other, although understandable, served as a block, a barrier to integrating with other students. Their chairs touched when they sat. They often walked arm in arm. They laughed at the same time and stopped laughing at the same time. There was never an opening for anyone else.

Then one morning the smiles and laughter vanished, replaced with teary, red, swollen eyes and handkerchiefs held to snotty noses. A heavy sadness blanketed the classroom. Sitting around our big table, the kids, signaling with their eyes, silently directed my attention to Jiao, the seventh-grade girl. She had broken into another round of tears. The younger one looked equally pained as she stared at her beloved sister with wide eyes and quivering lips. I attributed the genuine empathy of the class to the rawness of the girls' emotions.

My investigation began in earnest. Due to language issues, getting to the root cause of a disagreement or fight between kids required persistence. I had to rely on my students who spoke more English. Yet their information was often secondhand, and their conclusions were usually based on the victim's side of the story, intertwined with their own opinions of what had happened. These interpreters hadn't necessarily witnessed the event. Fortunately in the case of the sisters, the brief scene that emerged from the spotty input and multiple descriptions seemed believable, almost classic by nature.

Candelaria, a fourth-period student, bravely reported, "That big girl. Stephanie. She tell the China girl, 'I gonna beat you.'" This sparked a long session of passionate commentary. Even *I* knew of Stephanie—and I didn't teach her. A seventh-grader who weighed probably 180 pounds, she loomed over most of the students and even some of the male teachers. She lived for a fight, and all the kids, including boys, stayed clear of her. An overwhelmed grandmother was raising her, her mother was incarcerated, and Stephanie herself already had a juvenile record and a probation officer.

"So, Stephanie threatened Jiao," I clarified.

"Yes, and she pull the hair and push her," added Candelaria, pulling her own braid and pushing an imaginary someone down to demonstrate.

"Where did Stephanie do this?" I asked, even though I already knew the answer: in the girls' locker room before, during, or after a P.E. class. The sheer number of students assigned to those classes, compounded by the fact that different sets of students were clustered together who ordinarily weren't, made them a breeding ground for clashes.

"So it happened this morning in P.E.," I said, confused because I thought Jiao and her sister had P.E. in the afternoon.

"Yes, in P.E. Yesterday," Elicia responded, also confused by what "this morning" meant.

"Today or yesterday?" I pressed.

"Yesterday," Saúl confirmed. "Eight period."

The time frame of the story especially alarmed me. I knew Jiao's tears weren't fresh, which meant she wasn't reacting to something that had occurred minutes or even hours ago. She'd had an entire night to process her emotions.

A voice inside me hinted at a train wreck waiting to happen. But I ignored the voice, ignored the hints. I wanted to give everyone the benefit of the doubt, including Stephanie. *Maybe Jiao had overreacted, intimidated by Stephanie's size and rough demeanor*, I told myself. *Or maybe I'm not getting the whole story.*

As soon as I had a free moment, I paid a visit to Mr. Nickerson, head of student discipline. A slight man, he was difficult to find in his tiny, nondescript office. Like Waldo meandering through an office supply store, Mr. Nickerson sat somewhere amidst stacks two and three feet high of duplicate sheets of paper. Some stacks contained completed copies of forms, while others remained unused, wrapped in their cellophane coating. Stacks rested on the floor, on the window ledge, on his desk. I followed the white curly phone cord to find him, receiver in one ear, pencil behind the other, filling out a form on his typewriter, which barely fit in the center of his desk. I knew he spent most workdays sifting through endless documentation of student infractions and designating some semblance of consequence for each one. Yet, despite the stressful nature of his work, he came across as surprisingly cheery.

Mr. Nickerson ended the phone call and motioned me to sit down. I relayed everything I knew of the incident in the girls' locker room. He listened attentively, his eyes widening at the first mention of Stephanie, giving me a "yeah" every so often.

But before he had a chance to respond, the phone started ringing. He stared at it while he continued to ponder our conversation. Then he shook his head and, picking up the receiver, said to me, "I'm sorry. I have to take this call. I'll speak to the P.E. teacher this afternoon. If Stephanie's there, he absolutely *cannot* leave that locker room unattended even for a minute."

I left, feeling a familiar disappointment. Another incident, probably of a sudden development, once again had taken precedence.

The dreaded outcome involving the two sisters happened a few weeks later. Alone in my classroom during a planning period, I was busy creating posters for the next class. My door stayed open at this time of day since the hallway was pleasantly quiet. Hearing the random noises out there—a door being locked or unlocked, a distant conversation, the slam of a locker as a tardy student ran past—connected me to the comings and goings of the school.

As I worked, I registered a familiar sound: a key turning in the exterior double doors at the end of the hallway, doors leading to the back building that housed the offices of Mr. Nickerson and the two assistant principals. The doors banged shut, followed by the increasingly louder *tap-tap-tap* of high heels and the jingling of keys. I assumed that Ms. Meyer, the assistant principal, was making her daily rounds. Yet today the echo of her tapping heels and jingling keys didn't fade once she'd passed my classroom. Instead, her shoes slowed at my door, marched into the room, and continued toward me, sitting undisturbed at my work table. The woman's purposeful stride caused my skin to tingle and my pulse to quicken.

I liked and admired Ms. Meyer. But during my three years at the school, we'd never held a private conversation except in passing. She and I were two of four white staff members. The remaining seventy-plus members were Black. In her fifties, Ms. Meyer dressed exquisitely in expensive, colorful suits that contrasted well with her thick auburn hair. Her sense of style had earned her a certain respect in a community that valued dress and presentation. She also maintained a reputation for courteousness by making it a point not to offend.

"The two girls from China withdrew this morning," the assistant principal said in a professional, unemotional manner. She stood facing me on the opposite side of the large table. Her red-painted nails gripped her walkie-talkie to turn down the volume in case it exploded with static. "The older one got beat up pretty badly in the shower yesterday," she continued. "Stephanie did it. It was bad."

There was a thoughtful pause, as if she was deciding where to take the conversation next. Ms. Meyer had been at this a long time, soon to retire. I looked to her for cues. The scenario was a can of worms that could be opened or left closed. At this point, what good would come of acknowledging the school's failure to protect? Or, maybe the pause signified that the situation had saddened us both so much that we had no energy for words.

I did appreciate her coming directly to me so I wouldn't have to learn the news from the kids. In another setting we might have launched into a heartfelt talk. But I had a class in ten minutes and she had lunch duty.

"Well." Ms. Meyer raised an arm then quickly lowered it, as if to say, *It is what it is*.

I switched course. "What school did they transfer to?"

"They didn't say," she replied. "The father came this morning and filled out the paperwork. The girls weren't with him."

"And what about Stephanie?"

"Oh, she's in juvenile. You know her mama's been in prison a while. Stephanie's hearing will be in a week or so . . ." Her voice trailed off.

I'll never see those girls again, I thought with sorrow. And Stephanie being further rooted in the criminal justice system added another layer of despair.

So much to say. But we said nothing.

"Okay. I just wanted to let you know firsthand what transpired," Ms. Meyer said. She turned and walked out the door. I listened to the new echoes of her heels bouncing off the walls of the hallway. In the silence that returned, I sat with my thoughts. Then I slowly came to, gathered and put away my markers and poster board, wrote the date on the blackboard.

Students solemnly trickled in, aware of the fate of their Chinese classmates. The two empty seats loomed large, as if a spotlight shone on them, as if they were glaring reminders of life's harsh realities.

I began the class with an announcement that the sisters had left the school. Slowly, one by one the students started to talk about it. Since some were more informed than others, this evolved into a genuine give-and-take conversation. The speakers and the listeners assumed their roles naturally. One of the few positive aspects of traumatic events within a school was that they provided fodder for opportunities to practice speaking English. The students' closeness to the shared experience heightened their incentive to communicate.

Taking advantage of their level of motivation, I improvised forty minutes of focused repeating, paraphrasing, and acquiring much-needed vocabulary. The lesson ended with each student writing farewell notes to the sisters to express their sentiments. Inspiration to communicate had carried through to the writing. They went back and forth to the pencil sharpener, consulted their dictionaries, helped each other with spelling, even read their sentences out loud without any prompting from me.

Then, unprompted by me as well, they launched into creating something worthy of conveying their farewell notes: handmade cards. The girls' cards—with their pink cutout hearts, red roses, and glittered *I Love You*'s and *I Miss*

You's—outdid those the boys made. Yet even my toughest male students' creations featured Valentine stickers and their best cursive.

Finally, I circled the classroom, holding open a large envelope. They ceremoniously inserted their cards, notes tucked inside, as if parting forever with some treasured heirloom. A few of the girls hesitated then kissed their cards as they mournfully let them go. The room reeked of Elmer's glue and Sharpie ink. I promised the class I'd bring the envelope to the front office before leaving school so it could be mailed right away to the girls' home.

But I never sent anything. The family hadn't left a forwarding address or the name of the school of transfer. The sisters' light, sweet spirits dissipated like a narrow funnel cloud, out through the cracks in our classroom window, into the thick humid air and, hopefully, to some safer part of the big city. The card collection remained stuffed in a cabinet in my classroom, hidden from students' view.

The assault of Jiao occurred years ago. Nowadays, schools have additional methods at their disposal to prevent such incidents: hidden cameras; adults hired to monitor hallways, stairwells, and shower rooms; "Zero Tolerance" and "No Place for Hate" programs; peer mediation and mentoring programs; and support groups for kids of incarcerated parents. Yet the fact remains that public schools don't get to choose their students. They have to accept whoever walks through the door with proof of residence, regardless of the child's history of crime or violence. If enough Stephanies enroll in a school, then that school suffers safety challenges. There's no way around it.

Teachers are stepping-stones. They rarely learn of their students' future failures and achievements. They don't get to see the outcomes. I prayed that the Chinese sisters' difficult introduction to American schools didn't scar them for life. I dared to believe that it served only as a small setback on a road leading to some degree of happiness and success.

Unexpected Disclosure

The kids wore their coats and jackets inside the warm portable as we awaited a few latecomers for our departure to the Mexic-Arte Museum. The classroom buzzed like a predawn Christmas morning—a bit of pandemonium, hyper chatter, children who could hardly contain themselves. My students appreciated an opportunity to escape the campus for a morning, or afternoon, or a full-day field trip. They welcomed a break from the monotony of rules, bells and whistles, lunch in the sterile cafeteria, the strangeness of English spoken at every turn. They cherished adventure and time together. I sat at my desk and once again counted the students in the room and then the coffee-stained, signed permission slips stacked on my desk. The totals had to match.

As usual on days with a morning field trip, I purposely stretched the wait time. I did it for those kids who, for whatever reason, hadn't yet turned in their permission slips, who had looked so forlorn the day before, vowing they'd show up extra early the day of the outing, required signature in hand.

Magaly was one such student. She burst through the door in her church-donated long tweed coat that could be mistaken for no one else's. Its solid hot-pink color contrasted brilliantly with the light, form-fitting black hoodies most of her peers sported.

"Magaly's here! Yay! Magaly can come!" her girlfriends cried, jumping for joy. Then they danced in a tight circle, the in-out-in-out movement of their chins reminiscent of barnyard chickens. The source of their happiness rushed to my desk as I stuffed the last of the paperwork into a worn manila envelope. The ground under her patent leather shoes practically vibrated with delight.

"Ms. Smith, my mom say yes, I can go with you to the museum," she announced breathlessly, beaming with pride. Her small hand let go of the crinkled paper as she returned to high-five each of her friends.

Like a child granted the freedom to play outside after being confined to her room for days, Magaly, with her school chums at her side, exuded curiosity and joy during the entire excursion. It began with her surging to the front of the pack, swinging hands with different comrades on our eight-city-block walk to the downtown museum. While we were there, she lingered among the Día de los Muertos altars, noting each type of fruit, each fabric of bedazzling colors, each black-and-white photo. At our McDonald's lunch stop, she barely finished her small order of fries from so much giggling and having to hold her sides. Later, on the city bus taking us back to the campus, she mobilized students to break out in song, prompting a round of applause from random passengers.

That Magaly's parents had agreed to let her participate in the field trip was highly unusual. As Jehovah's Witnesses, they forbade their daughter from partaking in holiday activities—wearing a costume for Halloween, exchanging Secret Santa gifts or seeing special light displays around Christmas. An undercurrent of parental disdain for fun seemed to follow her; and as Magaly settled into adolescence, an element of parental distrust also developed. Anytime she stayed after school, I had to vouch for her whereabouts by either signing a paper she took home or speaking directly on the phone to a parent. On more than one occasion, her mother stopped by my portable on her way to or from work to request a printed copy of Magaly's grades, as if she needed proof beyond her daughter's word.

Magaly's attitude toward her religious restrictions impressed me. She never complained or gave out any hint of irritation at, for example, having to spend Saturdays at church or knocking on strangers' doors to find souls to convert. At school she refrained from righteous speeches about Jesus or the Bible, nor did she seem to judge others' behaviors.

Magaly stood out from the middle-school crowd in many ways, yet remained comfortable in her own skin. For one thing, she'd immigrated to Texas from Guatemala with her adopted family, a fact she was very upfront about. In a setting where most of the students were of Mexican heritage, staff and students sometimes mistook Magaly for Mexican. This hurt her feelings. Fiercely proud of her country, she adorned herself daily with something representative of her *patria*—the colors of Guatemala's flag, or a Guatemalan national soccer player's jersey, or a wristband or barrette woven with an indigenous pattern.

It was her physical characteristics that set her apart. Her perfectly straight white teeth contrasted beautifully with her cinnamon-colored skin. Her diminutive height and large, almond-shaped brown eyes were signs of her Mayan descent. The girls in her age group dedicated themselves to long, silky, straight hair, yet Magaly's fell inches above her shoulders in natural curly locks that were rare among people of like descent.

Her voice distinguished her more than any other attribute. It was so hoarse and gravelly that when I first met her I assumed she'd recently been in a shouting match on the playground. From then on, I could close my eyes at any given moment and tell that it was Magaly speaking.

"Ms. Smith," Magaly said, standing beside my desk. "Ms. Marquez let me come here for the whole period. I already finish my work of science yesterday in her class. Can I help you, please? I be very quiet. I tell the kids to listen." Magaly's ESL class had ended less than twenty minutes ago, and yet now she was returning to my portable for another seventy. My domain had become her domain, and I allowed it because she epitomized the assistant every teacher dreamed of.

"Did Ms. Marquez write you a pass?" I asked, as always. I worried that Magaly spent too much time in my ESL classroom and too little on science instruction.

"Ye-e-s, of course," she said, placating me as she dug around in the front pocket of her backpack. We both knew that by the time she located the crumpled pass, I would have forgotten about wanting to see it.

A future teacher, she needed no guidance. Magaly immediately plunked down a chair by the three brand spanking new arrivals from Guatemala. Checking their pencil points, she shook her head in disapproval then gathered their pencils and took them to the sharpener. The Guatemalans half smiled, glad to have someone running interference.

Next, she checked their papers for proper headings. *"No. No. Así no. Hay que escribir la fecha al lado derecho."* She was gently scolding them for failing to write the date on the right-hand side of the page. Then she held up her own, correct example. She'd remembered my emphasis at the start of the school year on this minor detail. I felt heartened that she wanted to equip "her students" with my standard conventions. Introducing basic procedures such as where to include the date eased them into the huge learning curve that lay ahead. They eagerly copied Magaly's heading example onto a new sheet of ruled paper, eyeing each item line by line.

The three newcomers latched onto Magaly like

baby chicks to a mother hen. When the class prepared to transition to the computer lab for the remaining twenty minutes, Magaly reminded me that her small entourage needed a head start since their computer skills would call for major attention. They might have come from a Guatemalan village with sketchy internet service, or none at all. After I quietly signaled Magaly to go ahead, they slipped out of the classroom unnoticed. By the time the other students reached the lab, the newbies had entered all their personal identification information necessary to register with the school server.

In a matter of days, the computer-illiterate newcomers learned to create and save documents and files and to use Google's translator, all due to Magaly's intense direction. I felt especially indebted to her when she braved instructing the three of them to use the cumbersome bilingual dictionary written in tiny print. Constrained by her own lack of reading skills, she demonstrated rather than explained a word search—which often took a while. Her audience observed unblinkingly, looking off only once or twice while they shifted their feet or coughed softly, as Magaly scanned page after page in her search for that all-important vocabulary word. Eyeing the mini-lesson from across the room, I smiled to myself. My belief that kids reinforce newly learned skills through teaching them was ringing loud and clear.

A huge challenge for new immigrant students involved getting free lunch in the cafeteria while fifty squirmy, hungry preteens stood behind them in line. Students entitled to free lunch punched their seven-digit student ID into a tiny device by the cash register. For most, their ID numbers had traveled with them since kindergarten, so the process was almost instantaneous. But not for the newcomers. Again, Magaly anticipated this difficulty, most likely from firsthand experience, and accompanied the three Guatemalans through the lunch line their first week. Like a true teacher, she insisted that they themselves punch in their numbers so as to get adequate practice and become independent. And she didn't hesitate to quiet or even elbow impatient bystanders who griped about the Guatemalans slowing things down. "Oh my God," she'd shout. "What wrong with you? They new and don't understand. *Paciencia.*" Then she'd turn back to her "trainees" and say, "Don't listen to those *tontos*. They silly. They can wait." As petite as Magaly was, something about her commanded respect. She possessed a knack for waging battles against injustices. And she called out both friend and foe if they wronged someone.

Not one to break rules, she made sure her three minions didn't get into trouble. One morning after students had begun the warm-up, she motioned for me to step outside. "Miss," she said under her breath, "you see the *camisa* of Elena?" Student outfits weren't on my morning radar as they should have been, so I stepped back inside the portable to have a look. Sure enough, Elena's shoulders were exposed as she bent over her writing, and her spaghetti-strap shirt, actually a camisole, barely covered her cleavage. Elena had clearly violated the school dress code, though probably not out of defiance. More likely, no one had explained to her what she could and couldn't wear.

"Miss." Magaly was fretting and pulling my arm. "I have to take her right now to CIS [the Communities in Schools office]. She have to change. We can get a *camiseta* in there. If she don't go now, the office send her home."

"Calm down. Elena can put her jacket back on to walk to CIS," I told Magaly, trying to address her sense of urgency. "I'll write you a pass to take her."

"Ms. Smith," Magaly hissed, "why she take off her jacket before? She don't understand." She shook her head, mortified by her friend. Then she quietly walked over to Elena, tapped on her bare shoulder, and signaled the girl to follow her. Thirty minutes later they returned, Elena wearing an oversized Bugs Bunny T-shirt.

"Look, everybody," Magaly announced, laughing.

"Elena has Bugs Bunny."

Magaly and Looney Tunes had rescued Elena from the drama of being suspended.

Whoever gained Magaly's loyalty—newcomer, classmate, friend, or teacher—ultimately benefited. She served as helper and guide, but also as protector and defender. Magaly's undying devotion to me had to do with the students I taught. Being an immigrant was a strong part of her identity. And she bonded with all other immigrants and refugees, not just Guatemalans. My classroom symbolized a refuge, existing exclusively for students like her, set apart from the rest of the campus. I became an extension of that refuge.

She sometimes came to my defense, averting a mini-mutiny with her catchphrase "Come on, guys." For instance, during one difficult class, students banded together in resistance to my latest writing assignment. Magaly sat back in her chair and observed silently until she could no longer tolerate the discussion. "Guys, Ms. Smith trying to teach English to us. You not want learn English?" she lectured indignantly, hands on hips.

"Oh, Magaly, shut up. You not my teacher," Soe Lin countered good-naturedly, although he, as did other boys, seemed to take pleasure in squashing her authority.

Miguel Ángel always had the strongest reaction to Magaly's outbursts. That particular day he told her, "Why you so mad? You can do your work. Go ahead. Mind your business. You can't tell nobody what to do."

"Miguel Ángel," Magaly yelled, her agitated, hoarse voice sounding like the weak intermittent signals of a radio. "You just lazy. You never do work. You think is too hard but is not. You can do it, Miguel Ángel. Just try."

"I know English not hard. Is easy for me. Is hard for you. I already know English," he boasted.

"Miguel Ángel, you crazy." Magaly sounded despondent, knowing the futility of arguing with him. Yet eventually, between her goading, a few others' goading, and

75

my own, the class settled into writing.

Miguel Ángel's comment about English being hard for Magaly struck a chord. Language acquisition *didn't* come easily to her, yet Magaly proved relentless in her commitment to learning it. She, like the others, didn't initially welcome challenge. Sometimes her body language indicated defeat: shoulders slumping, head laid on the table, or face covered by hands. Yet before long she'd rise to the occasion, deflect the negative energy, walk into the line of fire. She'd gear up to do whatever was required, then encourage others to join her. The first to start writing, to skim the text, to ask a pertinent question, she pushed on.

On days when I shifted into my taskmaster mode, demanding that students repeat phrases with perfect accuracy, Magaly persisted. When I refused to move on until two or three students had produced the random sentence, she was the volunteer who stumbled, starting over and over, until she uttered the lengthy stream of words to my satisfaction. She validated the notion that expertise is more likely to result from practice and discipline than from natural talent. During her middle-school years, she blossomed into a solid English speaker, reader, and writer.

Language might not have been Magaly's strong point, but math and science undoubtedly were. Talking with her teachers, I discovered, much to my relief, that she was a whiz in both subjects—which is why her science teacher allowed her to miss so much class time. She was living proof that many learners exhibit strengths in some content areas and weaknesses in others.

My most vivid memory of Magaly is when she revealed the tragic story of her biological mother. As usual, she came to my portable carrying a lunch tray from the cafeteria. But this day she didn't arrive with her entourage of girlfriends, some of them my students and some not. I sat at my desk eating lunch and checking emails. She understood that I valued my free time, and that I didn't object to students eating lunch or hanging out before school in my portable, provided they didn't make too much noise or mess.

We chitchatted as Magaly nibbled at pizza and applesauce and I ate my cheese sandwich. Then she slid her tray holding the barely touched food to one side and politely asked to use a computer. Students had to first eat at the tables and wipe their hands before going to the computer station. Noticing how little they sometimes consumed, I wondered if this rule had an adverse effect. Many of them didn't have a working computer and internet service at home. I hated to think that during their thirty-minute lunch hour they felt obliged to choose between eating and computer time.

I glanced in Magaly's direction while she arranged herself. I admired her patient, methodical maneuverings— repositioning the monitor with both hands, centering the keyboard, brushing crumbs and dust off the table. Such a contrast with my frantic clicking. Like the mother of a large brood who unexpectedly finds herself alone with one of them, I willed myself to continue observing Magaly. She checked her emails and then, as all the girls did, turned to a popular fashion game. She clicked and dragged clothing and jewelry selections over to a Barbie doll-looking figure. The game seemed ill suited for Magaly, too childlike for the mature thirteen-year-old that she was. But I remembered my own collection of paper dolls I'd enjoyed up until seventh grade. My heart warmed as I realized that adolescence still embodied a rare blend of lingering and emerging behaviors.

I asked her if she wouldn't mind setting up my computer for the next class since she knew exactly what to do. I went to the printer to retrieve a document. Waiting as the green printer light blinked, chin resting on elbow, I attempted a conversation. For the past few weeks my voice had been hoarse due to a combination of allergies, talking too much and too loudly, and exhaustion. "Magaly," I said offhandedly, "my voice sounds like yours now. I'm glad. I like your voice. Why *is* your voice like that? Why is your voice so rough?" (She wouldn't have understood *hoarse*.)

Staring ahead at the computer screen, she informed me in a tone she might have used to name what she'd eaten for breakfast, "When I was a baby, very little, my real mom she try to kill me. Like this." She placed her hands around her neck and pantomimed gasping for air. "So my voice like this now."

"Your mom tried to choke you? To *suffocate* you?" The words tumbled out of my mouth. I couldn't think fast enough.

Magaly nodded. "My mom try to suf-suf . . ." She did her best to repeat the new word, but the three syllables proved too hard. Silence.

Large teardrops slid down her cheeks. I grasped for some sort of explanation, one she could understand, given the language gap. "Maybe your mom had that sickness. Some women have it right after they have a baby. It's a kind of depression. It can make them do crazy things."

"Yes, I know." The bubbly tone she was attempting was heartrendingly forced.

"Magaly, you know it's not that your mother didn't love you. I'm sure she loved you," I consoled. I hoped she'd heard about the condition and wasn't simply appeasing me.

"When I go to my country, I can see my mom." She'd bounced back, almost smiling. Once again, I recognized how a sad situation was intensified for an immigrant or refugee. Magaly's separation from her mother not only had happened soon after her birth, but it also had entailed a great physical distance, and borders, and different languages and cultures. She clearly longed to meet her mother again, and yet the likelihood of a reunion was miniscule.

"Oh, you know where your real mother lives?" I asked, wanting to sound positive.

"Yes," she replied.

I wondered if her adopted family was blood-related but refrained from asking. She'd divulged enough. "Maybe you can write letters to her?" I suggested.

"No. My mom don't read Spanish. No school. And her language, I can't write." She paused. "Is okay. One day I see her. I talk to her," Magaly reassured me. Her willingness to connect with her grief had passed.

The bell rang, pulling us back into our seemingly trivial routines. I reiterated how sorry I was. "Is okay," she said one last time in her gravelly, cheerful voice then left the room carrying her lunch tray.

Magaly never broached the subject again. I did, but not with her. I shared that unexpected disclosure with her science and math teachers, who loved her as much as I did.

For months, I struggled to reconcile my image of the grounded, confident, well-adjusted Magaly with the young girl who carried in her heart such a painful reality, her voice serving as a daily reminder. I concluded that the mystery of resilience was alive and well in my classroom.

Some children suffer at the hands of bullies yet miraculously don't become bullies themselves. Other children sit in disruptive classrooms with fraught teachers who can barely teach, and yet, somehow, they come away with new knowledge. Still others grow up in homes with abusive, narcissistic parents, the most negative role-modeling, yet end up successful individuals on many fronts.

Resilience is bittersweet: sad but encouraging, tragic but hopeful. After seeing the resilience of my students, I was less afraid of making mistakes, less anxious about botched opportunities to help a child succeed. I moved forward, a slightly lighter step to my gait.

Gone Fishing

Youssouf Fofana and his older brother Momolu were the only students I ever taught from Liberia. They joined the class after the winter break—radiant spirits with shiny shaved heads, bringing an energy that seemed to flood the school gates, both of them bursting through on a mission to forge friendships, learn English, and play soccer, marbles, or whatever game happened to be at the forefront. Unfortunately, their peers in my ESL classroom didn't readily embrace them. Slowly but surely, in various subtle and not-so-subtle ways they were rebuffed. Like the sail of a boat that loses its guiding wind, the brothers' joyful energy sagged soon enough.

The year the Liberian brothers entered my class, enrollment consisted mainly of Latin Americans—from Cuba, Honduras, Guatemala, and Mexico. They were Spanish-speaking and predominantly Catholic. Youssouf and Momolu spoke Gola, a tribal African language, and were Muslim. The students from Latin America all happened to be relatively light-complexioned that year, while Youssouf and Momolu were dark-complexioned. The Latin Americans were considered immigrants, while

Youssouf and Momolu's family was considered refugees. This last distinction had made their journey to the United States very different. Many of the Latin Americans had crossed the border with strangers or with a single relative to rejoin family members. The Fofana family arrived by plane, intact, greeted by members of a local church who served as advocates during the assimilation period. The immigrant students had experienced upheaval in the form of leaving behind family members or crossing the border illegally or both. Youssouf and Momolu's trauma lay not in a risky journey to the United States, but in previously having escaped war, hunger, and death in their native country, then surviving in a refugee camp.

Youssouf had certain strikes against him. He emitted a forcefulness that was off-putting to his peers. They found his way of talking to be too loud and his sense of personal space intrusive. Day after day I watched Youssouf pine for companionship, bouncing a basketball by himself during break time, singing a tune that caused everyone to cover their ears and yell, "Stop!" It made my heart ache, and when I could stand it no longer I, along with Mr. Keaton, the sixth-grade counselor, began to plot an intervention of sorts.

One morning the counselor abruptly snuck into the classroom, turned off the lights, and closed the door. "Freeze, everybody! You're all under arrest!" he shouted, grabbing pretend guns from his pretend gun holder. (This is something one would never do nowadays in a school setting.) It was three quarters of the way through class, fifteen minutes remaining until lunch—and he immediately had everyone's attention.

"Si quieren almorzar, tienen que darme todo su dinero." Mr. Keaton, in his fluent Spanish so very appreciated by my students who spoke it, had told them that if they wanted to go to lunch later, they'd better give him all their moola.

Everyone knew Mr. Keaton for the trickster he was,

and the kids played along. Some gestured shooting back at him, while others faked reaching for cash. Youssouf couldn't contain himself. Driven by his passionate nature that often transgressed into the overzealous, he raced over to high-five Mr. Keaton, who he adored.

"*¡Perfecto!*" exclaimed Mr. Keaton, taking Youssouf by the shoulders. *"Aquí está el mismísimo caballero del que les voy a hablar."* The counselor's hands were on the shoulders of the very "gentleman" he was going to talk to my students about.

"And also about his brother over there in the corner," Mr. Keaton said in English, saluting Momolu who, unlike Youssouf, didn't like to be the center of attention. Momolu waved shyly, resting his head against the cement wall, his gold neck chain shining in the darkened room. "Ms. Smith and I have been banging our heads together"—he faked pounding his head on a wall while banging his feet for the sound effect—"wondering how we can get you all to be friends with these two guys. I mean, what do they have to do to impress you? Thirty push-ups?" Mr. Keaton plunged to the floor and did ten solid push-ups, counting with his fingers up in the air. Youssouf joined him.

The class roared in laughter. Hooting, clapping, fake booing. The counselor's energy infused the room. It rattled the doors and windows.

After clearing his throat dramatically for effect, Mr. Keaton switched back to Spanish. "Seriously, can you imagine not one other person in this school speaking your language? You all have each other. You're *COMPADRES*." This last word he yelled, planting his face smack in front of a student's, practically spitting on him. He paused and then paced, hands in his pockets. The audience quieted and followed his every move. "Who can Youssouf talk to but his sorry brother? Who wants to talk to a brother every minute of the day? Would you? Do you all love your brothers—or sisters—that much?" He banged his fist on an empty desk.

"There's more. What happens when you want some good Mexican food? Well, you students from Mexico have a choice of three restaurants on the very same street our school is on. In Austin, there are hundreds of Mexican restaurants." He made a dramatic sweep with his hand.

"But what about Youssouf and his brother?" This, Mr. Keaton said in English. "Where do *they* go for some good Liberian food? Home. That's right. Home to their apartment. There isn't a single Liberian place to eat in the whole city. Home can get boring, don't you think?"

Everyone (except the Fofana brothers) nodded, wide-eyed.

The counselor made a theatrical departure. A few minutes later, my students' exit to lunch was somber—unlike the usual pushing they did to be first in the cafeteria line.

After Mr. Keaton's inspiring delivery, I assumed Youssouf's and Momolu's social life would improve. But apparently I'd been the only one impressed by the counselor's performance. Momolu became prone to aggression and fights, while Youssouf continued to wander apart, lonely. As a teacher and an adult, I could encourage, cajole, scold, shame, and create opportunities for inclusivity. Yet, ultimately, young people decide for themselves who they're going to befriend. The Fofana brothers' situation brought me a dose of reality: the periodic harshness and mean-spiritedness of the middle-school years.

During my career I witnessed schools amp up efforts to encourage respect for diversity and inclusivity among students. This happened in response to the increase in teen suicides, hate crimes, and mass shootings. When I was teaching the Fofana brothers, the campus adopted the "No Place for Hate" campaign offered by the school district. As part of the campaign, a staff member spearheaded a student committee that attended trainings, then presented skits, slogans, role-plays, and chants to the student body. The idea was to teach ways to identify and minimize racism. In addition, during the students' advisory period (called "homeroom" in an earlier era), a curriculum was implemented that focused on anti-bullying techniques and conflict resolution skills. Although necessary and worthwhile, both the campaign and the curriculum seemed an oversimplification. They glossed over the immense courage needed to confront a bully or to stand up to a peer group, as well as the infrequency with which either of these things really happened. In other words, stopping negative behaviors isn't nearly as easy as it's sometimes made out to be.

Youssouf's predicament led me to consider human behavior in general: the tendency to stay in one's comfort zone, to resist the unfamiliar. I listened to psychologists denounce social media for bolstering users' control over who they associated with. Facebook, as an example, reinforced tendencies to communicate exclusively with like-minded people.

What became increasingly clear to me was that some adults realize they benefit from forging relationships with people who are different because such relationships satisfy and refresh. An exchange of values and skills takes place. Perspectives shift.

As in all matters related to encouraging positive behaviors among children, the real work for us grownups lies in leading by example in our own lives. Years before, I'd become friends with a teacher whose classroom was next to mine. We presented an unlikely pair, considering this was South Houston in 1997. He was from Alabama and I was from Connecticut. He was a Black man in his late twenties and I was a white woman ten years his senior. Mr. Collier and I shared two passions: teaching literature to reluctant readers; and social issues, which we conferred on as we stood at our respective classroom doors during passing periods. As well, the students often observed us in the hallways laughing, shaking our heads, even occasionally having heated discussions. They probably noticed us sharing books and magazine articles, or asking favors of each other like covering a class for the last fifteen minutes so the other one could make an after-school appointment on time. I believe our friendship ultimately made an impression on the school's homogeneous population, which was 97 percent Black.

With the spring break around the corner, and knowing that school vacations brought isolation and boredom for newly arrived students, I invited the Fofana brothers to spend a day of the five-day break at my house. Momolu had to work with his father, but Youssouf jumped at the chance. His family lived on a busy avenue spawning apartment complexes and strip malls. I lived outside the city in a rural area. Maybe the change of scenery would be good for him. Besides, my son Jonas was close enough in age to Youssouf that they might enjoy each other.

Since Youssouf's visit happened to fall on his first St. Patrick's Day in the United States, I made an early-morning run to the grocery store to buy the traditional four-leaf-clover-shaped cookies sprinkled green, napkins of the same color, and a grinning leprechaun balloon that I hoped wouldn't scare him. After racing back home, I prepared a festive welcome.

It was a perfect spring day—crystal-clear blue sky, cool and breezy. I knew I had the right apartment complex when I spotted Youssouf standing amidst the billowing flags on display at the entrance. He waved and smiled. His bright white teeth were hard to miss. No sooner had I seen him than a little boy riding a tricycle in the parking lot fell onto the pavement and began to cry. Youssouf ran to him, picked him up from the asphalt, and brushed off his knees. Once Youssouf determined he wasn't hurt, he stepped up to my minivan window and shouted over the little boy's shrieking,

"My brother Monty? He can come?"

"Ask your mother," I shouted back. I then noticed an elegant-looking African woman watching from an apartment doorway. Youssouf yelled to her in his language and she vigorously nodded. We all waved, nodded, smiled, as if in a silent motion picture. The boys piled in, so excited they forgot the tricycle in the middle of the parking lot until I directed Youssouf to put it on the sidewalk. They were a bundle of energy, and once again my son was going to spend time with kids he didn't know and couldn't communicate with. Yet I knew Jonas was captivated by their exuberance and the strange language in which they shouted to one another.

On the way home, I reflected on how happy the mom had looked. Secretly, I praised myself for possibly giving her a day of freedom from childcare. Also, I thought she might be grateful her sons would have an opportunity to play somewhere besides the parking lot or the occasional public park. Today was proving to be a win-win situation for everyone involved.

Once we neared the house, Youssouf and his brother, unaccustomed to the bumpy dirt roads, had to hold on to avoid hitting their heads on the minivan's ceiling. This seemed to animate them even more. Slowly the community lake came into view, glistening in the bright sunshine. Drawn to the wide-openness of the scene, I spontaneously parked the car, and Youssouf and Monty got out and rushed ahead to the water's edge. In that spot floated a pair of the largest turtles I'd ever seen in the lake. Almost two feet in diameter, the creatures most likely had emerged because of the lack of human activity and the warmth that emanated all around. Yet part of me wanted to believe they'd risen to the surface for Youssouf's sake—today being his lucky day. At least it was starting out that way. The two brothers hustled along and kicked the tall grass behind us, searching for sticks.

Youssouf pointed in the direction of the turtles. "In

my country, we eat. We can catch and eat?" He peered up at me sideways, squinting in the dazzling light. I paused, not wanting to disappoint so early during our time together. Jonas also narrowed his gaze at me, wondering how I'd explain my way out of this unexpected request.

"Oh, we don't eat these turtles. They're for the people who live here to enjoy. The people who come to this park to swim. And to, uh, watch the turtles. And the fish."

Youssouf looked around at all the invisible people. *Silly Americans*, I imagined him thinking, *always holding on to things they never use.* We headed back to the minivan, with its four doors left open, making it appear perched and about to topple over.

We bounced and jerked our way around a bend, then entered my gravel driveway canopied by oak trees. The boys leapt out before I had a chance to shift into park. "This is a forest!" Youssouf announced with authority. They both spun around several times, looking up at the dappled light filtering through the treetops.

The brothers' sweet enthusiasm triggered the regret I often felt over a lifestyle spent rushing from car to home, car to school, car to playdate, etc.—always the sense of hurrying to be inside. Youssouf and Monty remained in the yard in awe of the trees' simple beauty. I remembered the St. Patrick's Day balloon, napkins, and cookies I'd set out in the kitchen, just steps away from where we were. Then I smiled, appreciating that those things would most likely be overlooked by my guests.

Eventually we did go inside, and the two visitors immediately took the liberty of roaming from room to room through my newly constructed house. The drywall hadn't been put up yet, and so the divisions between rooms weren't clearly marked. Again, Youssouf offered his strong opinion: "You live in a castle!" I was touched that he felt this way about my modest, unfinished home.

Another animal sighting—my son's gerbils in his

bedroom. I couldn't tell if the tiny rodents had been seen first or heard first as they rummaged among the newspaper shavings at the bottom of the cage and rotated their miniature Ferris wheel. Surprisingly, the Fofana brothers asked similar questions about the gerbils as they had about the turtles. "Did you catch them? Are you going to eat them?" Jonas couldn't stop himself from giggling.

Had they starved in the refugee camp? They'd now associated with food two species of animals I considered pets. It dawned on me that it was probably unheard of in Liberia, or in many countries for that matter, to keep animals in a cage around your home if you didn't intend to eat them. Suddenly I cherished the idea that moments of enlightenment were in store for all parties involved today, not just Youssouf and Monty.

By now, the boys' exploratory natures determined where we headed next. Out the door they ran to the backyard. Jonas and I scurried to keep up. My property bordered a cattle ranch, the chicken-wire fence separating our yard from grazing cattle invisible in the relentless sunshine. Youssouf held his hand above his eyes, scouting the boundless Texas sky and land. He looked the part of the Lone Ranger on his horse, searching the horizon for outlaws. Yet given his previous reactions to turtles and gerbils, he was more likely to be searching for wild game than humans.

"Over there is a river," I told the boys and pointed to the end of the property, where it dropped off to a shallow creek. I purposely used the word *river* because *creek* wasn't in Youssouf's vocabulary.

"River?" Youssouf repeated. "Can we fish?" Of course, fishing. How could I have overlooked such an appropriate activity? I had no idea if or where we kept fishing rods. So I yelled to my husband, who had followed us outside and was standing on the back deck, "Do you think the boys could try fishing?"

"Well, no. That ain't going to work," he responded

in the southern drawl he tended to use when in doubt. "We don't have any bait. And it'd be too much trouble. You know, take too long to get everyone on the road and go buy some. And you definitely need bait to catch fish."

"Bait," Youssouf repeated. "What is bait?" While my husband gave a rundown of reasons not to fish, Youssouf disappeared into the toolshed. A minute later he was making a beeline for the creek with two shovels, one in each hand. Again, we trailed behind him, leaving my husband pacing on the deck. The voice of the naysayer quickly faded due to distance and the roar of the March wind.

What I next observed transported me—and probably my son, also observing—to a different time and place. The two brothers easily positioned themselves on an angled area of the sandstone bank not far above the creek. They began pounding the sandstone with the backs of the shovels. With each strike of the metal, the clamor grew louder and their speech grew faster. Since I had no clue as to what they were saying, Youssouf and Monty *seemed* to be agitated. But within seconds it all made sense. Small worms, ten or twenty, suddenly appeared against the sandstone rock. The boys pitched the shovels. Four small hands grabbed the squirming worms, yanking them from tiny holes in the rock. I ran the roughly hundred yards back to my kitchen to grab a container. A wasted effort on my part, since when I returned several minutes later with a yogurt tub, the worms had rolled up, lying comfortably in their cupped hands.

Observing the boys made me think about the currently popular notion of "outdoor education." Youssouf clearly loved seeing the lake, the trees that he referred to as a forest, and the creek. His appreciation of nature energized him and those around him. Nature captures children in ways that a classroom can't: it's one thing to read about a creek; it's something entirely different to wade in one.

I thought back to when I'd read a test passage with eighth-graders who struggled with the word *current*—as in a body of water. They couldn't grasp the meaning, critical to understanding the gist of the text, because they'd never swum in a river or a lake, only a swimming pool. The lack of knowledge about and appreciation for nature has become more prevalent among kids in general. What used to be their "outside time" is often taken up with being glued to electronic devices as they're chauffeured to and from school and their various activities. It's become a concern among child psychologists. To counterbalance it, some elementary schools have pushed for more outside recess time. Some middle schools have designated a specific number of advisory periods per month for outdoor activities. At any rate, here, at my house outside the city, one of my students, his little brother, my son, and I were—although not during actual school time—taking in the natural elements and all the surprises they never fail to offer.

The four of us passed the house on our way to the lake to fish. I insisted that the boys show my husband their "bait." They briefly opened their tightly closed fists filled with worms.

"Well, I'll be," my husband remarked, chuckling. "They showed me a thing or two. I'll fetch some twine to attach those worms to sticks. And find a few hooks." He rushed inside in search of more presumably pointless items. The naysayer seemed thrilled to have an unexpected opportunity to go fishing.

And fish we did that glorious afternoon. I don't remember hooking a single trout or bass, but the actual catch wasn't the point. We tromped up and down the creek bed. Neighbors with young children joined us, and even my husband stuck around for most of the afternoon. The leprechaun balloon went largely unnoticed and the four-leaf-clover cookies uneaten. We stayed outside the entire day—no time for video games or Xbox or other indoor distractions.

Back at school after spring break, Youssouf bragged

to any classmate within earshot about his time at my house. They stared at him expressionless while he swelled with boastful joy. He laughed too hard and talked too extensively about the turtles and the worms and the fish. Maybe nobody believed him.

Youssouf's adventure seemed to hold zero significance until the afternoon a student commented to me, "Youssouf is your favorite. Why you not take me and Jaime to your house? No fair." There it was—the response I'd been secretly waiting for. Not because I wanted anyone to feel insignificant, but because I wanted some concession of Youssouf's proud adventure. I smiled at the student and told her my truth. "I took Youssouf to my house because he doesn't have any friends to hang out with. You have friends."

Youssouf eventually did blend in with the social fabric of the school. I like to think the survival skills he demonstrated that St. Patrick's Day transferred to other realms—a keen ability to make one's way in the world.

I was his teacher only for sixth grade. Then his family moved and he went to a different middle school. But the last word on him happened the year after his visit to my house.

On that day my administrator and I stood at the staff room's kitchen sink, rinsing our plastic lunch containers. "Do you remember a student by the name of Youssouf?" she said, taking me totally by surprise.

"Of course," I said, delighted.

"He ran up to me after the soccer game last night and asked if you were still teaching here. He plays for Kealing [a middle school in the same district]," she reported. "He asked me to tell you he says hello. He's still as adorable as ever, only bigger." She grinned. "And he's quite the soccer star."

Boy Under the Radar

Wait a minute. Where did he come from? And how long has he been here?

I did a double take, alarmed that school had been in session over a month and I didn't know all my students. I observed the unidentified fourteen-or-so-year-old comfortably occupying a seat and scribbling words from the whiteboard into a journal exactly as the others did. Something about him stopped me from approaching. Maybe it was his obvious intent to avoid eye contact. He had slipped in and gone unnoticed. An image popped into my head: the Tin Man, Scarecrow, and Lion, in stolen uniforms, sneaking into the Wicked Witch of the West's castle by joining the end of the guards' procession. (Just for the record, during my absence the week before, the substitute teacher had signed the student's enrollment papers but failed to inform me.)

Noé stayed in the shadows—at least during his first round of attending our school. At the onset of the daily speaking activity, when students arranged themselves in a close circle without the distraction of pencil and paper, he would arrive well before the others. He'd sit down in a straight-backed chair, hands folded in his lap, and wait patiently. As students joined the circle, Noé would scoot his chair back, signaling them to sit in front of him. By the time everybody was positioned and ready, I could barely find him among the group. The one time I started to call on him, he calmly lifted his palm to shoulder-level. Then he shook his head silently, intercepting my intent. Actually, he warded off attention from anybody, always with a simple hand gesture or an averting gaze. His sense of self-possession exuded a maturity, almost manhood, suggesting that he had a plan for himself.

Noé's reluctance to participate didn't deter his classmates from liking him. His ever-present grin hinted that he found everything they said or did amusing. This encouraged students to entertain him. They'd cast glances in his direction after popping some wisecrack or landing a wadded piece of paper squarely in the recycling container at the back of the room. With his watchful darting eyes, nothing escaped him.

I suspected that he carried a host of untold tales and life experiences. Ultimately my suspicions were confirmed. Once he'd eased into his true gregarious self, he offhandedly revealed that he had illegally crossed into the United States not once, but twice. The second time was after having returned to Honduras to pay his respects to his dying grandmother.

After the fact, his grandmother's dying did explain his disappearance. Yet at the time, Noé simply slipped from my class in much the same way he'd entered it. His name vanished from the roll. I never signed withdrawal papers or heard an official announcement or even a passing explanation among staff members. I assumed I'd been overlooked in the process and that Noé had transferred to another middle school. Or maybe to the high school. He did seem older.

Like a blip on a radar screen, Noé came and went within weeks. Gone for good . . . or so I thought.

One cold, rainy Saturday morning in January, I stood huddled under a single umbrella with my colleague, Daniel Kruger. We were watching our girls, outfitted in their royal-blue and white uniforms, sprint back and forth on the soccer field. Considering the miserable weather, the team had drawn an acceptable number of fans. With no bleachers to sit in, several parents stood on the sideline, the fathers with hands in their jean pockets, the mothers shivering and clutching their purses and diaper bags. Younger siblings outlined a slalom ski course as they looped around spectators. Older siblings shook their heads at missed passes.

Students, possibly boyfriends, gathered in clusters of two or three, still waking up. All in all, a silent crowd, except for the principal, who marched up and down the sideline yelling his usual exhortation: *"Marquen. Marquen."* He was telling the girls, inexperienced and mostly staying in a clump, to shadow opposing team members.

I kept an eye on the match while I took advantage of a rare opportunity to visit with Daniel, the ESL science and social studies teacher. In other words, we taught the same kids.

He leaned in and said, "Karen would be passing my class if she wasn't so busy playing soccer. She needs to come to tutoring." The subject of his complaint had just successfully headed the ball to reverse its direction.

"She does okay in my class, but, yeah, she could do better. On the other hand, look at how much fun she's having," I countered. Then, genuinely impressed by Karen's physical coordination, I added, "And she's good."

At that point I noticed an inconspicuous male student in a gray cotton hoody standing alone several feet in front of us. He turned around to look at Daniel and me, as if he'd recognized our voices and was satisfying his curiosity. We exchanged nods. His hood half covered his face.

I continued my conversation with Daniel until something dawned on me. "Isn't that one of ours?" I remarked, pointing discreetly to the ghostlike figure.

We inched our way toward him.

Daniel gently removed the boy's hood from behind. "Yes, I think you're right," he said and sighed.

The uncloaked Noé stood sheepishly before us. He'd intentionally remained in the periphery during his brief time at school, and here he was, back in the same on-the-edge-of-things groove. Now he stood face to face with two of his teachers, and I wondered if he felt like a long-lost fugitive who had grown tired of dodging and hiding. Something about Noé tugged at my heartstrings.

But why had he ventured out on a misty winter morning to a school event if he'd been truant for the last months? Out of defiance? Or did I sense shame—caught red-handed at a Saturday school-sponsored soccer game when he hadn't been attending school? Were his motives as simple as having a girlfriend, or someone he hoped to be his girlfriend, on the team? Better yet, was he yearning to return to school and hoping that today some adult would seek him out? My instinct told me that last scenario most likely hit the target.

Not wanting to put Noé on the offensive, I kept my eyes on the game when I asked him, as if it were an afterthought, "So, where did you go?"

Like me, he stared at the playing field. But out of the corner of my eye I observed his familiar grin. He mumbled something that escaped me.

"So, do you go to school now, or do you stay home?" I pressed for an answer.

Slowly, quietly, Noé responded while still locking his gaze on the players scrambling toward the opposing team's goal. "No. I not in school." Then he looked down at his feet, as if he'd confessed a regrettable sin.

His honesty had surprised me, and after floundering for a tactful response, I deferred to my colleague to handle the situation. The chance that two males would bond seemed more likely. Also, Daniel Kruger was more qualified than me for a few reasons. Besides being truly bilingual, he was also well known in the immigrant community—a key volunteer, possibly a board member, at a local immigrant and refugee service organization. As such, he may have been privy to information about Noé that I wasn't.

"Mi'jo, you know that you and your family could get into trouble," my colleague gently chided Noé in Spanish. "Here in the United States, you must go to school. It's not a choice."

Noé's back stiffened.

"I could contact the police today. And they'd soon appear at your apartment, serving your mom or dad or whoever's responsible for you with a ticket. And, by the way, this ticket isn't cheap. It's hundreds of dollars. But I'm simply trying to warn you—not threaten you."

Noé didn't respond. His usually merry eyes glazed over. He looked, unblinking, into the mist.

Daniel, hoping as I was to get a reaction from Noé, continued, "I don't want to get the police involved. But I will if you don't get back in school."

Noé faintly dipped his chin, as if to say he'd heard it all before. Daniel recounted another truancy case, but Noé's demeanor held firm. Eventually my colleague drifted into a conversation with other students and the few staff members who had showed up.

Whistles were blown simultaneously, then their shrill sound faded fast. The game ended in a tie. Players left the field, leaving an unobstructed view of the surrounding gray sky. Noé didn't budge from his spot, probably waiting for Daniel and me to make our exits so he could make his without being bothered by us again.

I turned to leave but in the next instant found myself making a last-ditch effort. I walked over to Noé and tapped his shoulder. "You need to come back to school," I whispered.

"Okay, Miss," he responded without resistance, yet also without inflection.

He seemed to mean well, but I doubted he would show up in my classroom in the near future.

I went about my Saturday and Sunday making a mental to-do list for the week ahead, putting Noé at the top of that list. I didn't want him placed on some administrative back burner but, truth be told, neither did I feel eager to report his situation. My faith in the established protocol wavered.

Fortunately, I never had to take *any* action. On Monday, as I stood at the classroom door greeting students, Noé strode in with the final group of boys. He rode on the heels of another to create more distance from me. When he passed by he was looking down, but his grin said everything. Either he winked or I imagined he did. My heart leapt. Yet I kept my end of our unspoken bargain. I wouldn't make a big deal of his return.

I closed the door and took cutout paper stars, part of my reward system, from a sweater pocket. In my usual fashion, I walked among the tables, putting them at the work spaces of students who began their warm-up promptly. When I reached Noé, I placed three blue stars along the top of his blank page, my sign of welcome. He quickly folded them in his wallet for safekeeping.

Noé returned to school with renewed focus. During the next year and a half, he became my most prized student. He registered as a seventh-grader even though he was fourteen. A savvy move on his part, it gave him an extra year to acquire English. I enjoyed observing his insatiable desire to learn. His willingness to show vulnerability—to be the first to blunder through an exercise without success and survive the embarrassment—inspired others to try. He loved English, but English didn't love him. Like many students from Honduras, where public schools offered sporadic instruction, his literacy skills suffered.

He assumed the role of enthusiast. During group activities, he put forth a lot of energy rallying his classmates. Still, his skill level hindered these efforts, and on bad days his behavior would abruptly shift from an infectious intensity to despondency. He'd stop directing, put his pencil down, and stare into space, overwhelmed when the task switched to writing. He couldn't keep pace. At times like this, his apparent mood shift would infect the group like a blown fuse, all momentum lost.

Regardless of his academic shortcomings, though, Noé had the necessary ingredients to prevail as a leader of his peers. Since he was self-assured and disarming, students listened to him, even the most stubborn.

Noé often came to my defense, and I cherished him for it. For instance, one morning he took on Victor. The belligerent seventh-grader was tapping his pencil on the table while repeating a popular rap song refrain ad nauseum. Nothing except side conversations annoyed me more when I held the attention of the whole class. Not wanting to allow Victor to interrupt the flow of my presentation, I first tried to get him to stop his percussion by glaring at him. When that didn't work, I positioned myself behind him as I kept talking. No luck there either.

"Dang, man," Noé said softly but deliberately. "Why you have to be like that?"

"Huh? Be like what?" Victor asked, with feigned ignorance. Avoiding Noé's inquisitive stare, he added amplifier sounds with his mouth to the rhythmic routine.

Noé persisted. "Dude, nobody want to hear that right now," he said calmly. "Ms. Smith trying to teach something important." Finally, Victor's performance subsided.

What Noé had most in his favor was Petra, the smartest, nicest, most popular ESL girl there. They became an item for an entire semester—a substantial amount of time for a middle-school romance. Their refreshing relationship didn't involve the usual strife or power struggles. They became king and queen, commanding the right combination of studiousness, kindness, and intelligence. I delighted in knowing that Noé's difficult transition to school life had paid off so well for him. He loved learning, his class-mates . . . in short, he loved school.

Yet his home life remained shrouded in mystery. He seemed to operate independently. Alone in the world. He seldom mentioned parents or family, only an older sister once or twice.

It wasn't until the end of his time in middle school that his personal situation became clear. Students had to complete a choice sheet, an individual academic plan for high school. The required form had to be turned in with a parent's or guardian's signature. Noé missed the deadline. He offered no explanation. A day later I reminded him that his choice sheet was late. He nodded but offered no excuse.

A few days later Noé came to my portable after the last bell. "Miss? My schedule? For the high school?" he asked anxiously. "Is too late?"

"I don't think it's too late," I encouraged him.

"But . . . maybe . . . I can't," he confessed, dropping down into the chair in front of my desk. His thin hands trembling, he struggled for the words that would explain his problem.

"Noé, you're not planning to go to high school?" I panicked, unable to mask my disappointment.

"No, Miss. No," he replied. "My mom. She the problem. She don' want me go to school no more." He paused, grasping for words. "She want me stop school and go to work. Then I make money. I can help pay the bills. That what she want for me . . ." His voice trailed off.

A sadness infused the air around us. Now I understood why he hadn't returned the choice sheet. His mother refused to sign it.

I hesitated then asked, "What kind of job does your mother want you to get?"

"Oh, roofer. You know. He make the roof for the house. I can work with my uncle," Noé answered, unenthused. He already envisioned his future: low wages, long hours, stifling Texas heat. I reminded Noé that sixteen was the legal dropout age.

"My mom, she don' care about that." He let escape a muffled laugh, dismissing my comment with a brush of his hand. Evidently laws didn't apply as far as his mother was concerned.

I rushed to judgment. "Does your mother work?" I asked, envisioning an evil, lazy woman watching *telenovelas*—soap operas—all day long with no remorse for her promising young son.

"Yeah," he said. "And my stepdad too. But we need more money."

I knew Noé was the only child in the household—an uncommon situation. My anger quickly abated, leaving me with the sinking frustration of knowing there were no simple, easy answers. Noé's mother was doing what she believed to be in the best interests of her family. Still, I offered to call her.

Surprisingly, he agreed to this. Agreed as if my suggestion had been the whole point of his after-school visit. He shook my hand and left.

That evening I phoned the number Noé had given me and, in broken Spanish, left a message. Steering clear of creating any tension, I simply invited his mother to come to the school to discuss her son's future. She never responded.

With Noé's input, our next step was to compose a note, which he took home. Again, no response.

In the end, he heeded my advice and turned in his choice sheet with a fake signature.

Struck by the unfairness of Noé's predicament, I recalled other students of mine, past and present, for whom it was the other way around. They would have jumped at the chance to quit school and work instead, but their parents hadn't allowed it. Educators spun in frenzied circles trying to help kids who had no intrinsic motivation to graduate, whereas Noé, who had all the motivation in the world, appeared to be left to his own devices.

During all my years of teaching, few kids fell between the cracks. But once in a while they did. Noé's name didn't appear on many spreadsheets. He didn't qualify as a "bubble kid," a student a few percentage points from passing the state exam who would be given an extra push with after-school tutoring. He didn't make any at-risk list for violent tendencies or incarceration. Educators stayed inundated with elaborate accountability systems: mission statements, data-driven spreadsheets, pages illustrated with bar graphs and line graphs showing the tiniest of upswings or downswings in students' progress—all focused on performance scores. Children became numbers. The danger of data was that it distracted educators from situations needing immediate attention, from things happening right under our noses. Noé, for example.

Noé *did* enroll in high school. I learned about him piecemeal through former students on their way to or from that school. Scooting by the security cameras, they popped into my portable and updated me on various peers. Then they popped back out, either running late to school or, thinking they'd spotted the campus officer turning the corner, to avoid a trespassing fine. I felt disappointed when they reported that Petra and Noé broke up. Her father was too strict and didn't approve of Noé. Plus, her family had moved and she was transferring to a high school farther south. *At least Noé didn't drop out when he lost Petra*, I told myself. He must be doing okay.

The next time I gave serious thought to Noé was two years later when he showed up again at my portable. The inconspicuous knock came during my planning period.

Thinking it was a colleague needing to decompress, or a messenger from the main office notifying me of a meeting about a student, I quickly opened the windowless metal door. Noé stood before me, wearing his same charming smile. "Remember me, Miss?" he asked shyly.

"Of course," I replied, motioning him inside. Fortunately, I didn't have a class needing my attention. I told him how much older he looked, more filled out. He blushed and said he was going to a gym. How were his classes? His grades? Did he have so-and-so for a teacher at the high school?

As we chatted, we both became aware that the last time we'd seen each other we could have never enjoyed this easy exchange. His English had improved drastically. When I commented on it, he said, beaming, "I learned English good 'cause of you, Miss. You're a good teacher."

He was the same thoughtful, considerate person.

As our conversation slowed, Noé didn't miss a beat. "Miss, can you do me a favor?" he asked, looking directly at me. He explained that his problem once again involved his mother. Only then did I recall that she hadn't wanted him to stay in school.

"My mom," he said. "There's, like, something wrong with her. Like, in the head." He made small circles in the air above his right ear. They were fighting over the same issue—she insisting that he quit school to earn money, Noé wanting to finish high school. He rested an arm flat on my desk. I thought at first that he wanted to arm wrestle. Then he showed me bruises where his mother had hit him.

"So, my mom, she kicked me out the house for not paying rent 'cause I can't." He shrugged. "No job."

"And your stepfather?" I asked.

"He's gone too. My mom is too crazy. She beat him too. I tell my mom talk to someone. Maybe a counselor? But she don' listen. She don' listen to nobody." He looked down at his hands. "I try to help her but . . ." Noé shook his head.

Once again, his pain penetrated the room.

I had a fleeting vision of inviting Noé to live with my son and me. I could transform my small office into a cozy bedroom. Drop him off at the local high school on my commute to work. Introduce him to well-to-do community members who could assist him financially.

As I listened, I was struck by his fortitude. Alone, without family, he'd endangered himself twice by leaving his country and making his way to Texas. He'd persisted in learning English, stayed in school despite pressure not to, and now lived with a mentally ill mother. At seventeen, instead of being angry at a parent who stifled his dreams, Noé showed compassion. He knew she needed help and that he couldn't help her.

I considered mental illness and how it puts any family in a state of crisis, regardless of economic status. Social stigma comes with the territory. Noé came from a third-world country that held different cultural norms. Being a poor immigrant in this country compounded his situation. And the real clincher? His isolation. As a relative newcomer, he'd had little time to build a community of support. Who knew how close a relationship he had with his stepfather, and no siblings lived at home. Finally, as if all this weren't enough, his lack of English fluency affected his ability and confidence to explore his options.

"I can stay with my sister and her husband. But they want money. They told me get a job. But only part-time. They want me stay in school. They think school is important for me." Noé explained all this, unaware of my sudden relief that he hadn't, as I'd been thinking, spent the night under a tree in a park.

I felt honored that I was the one he'd turned to. School seemed to be his sole resource, and he'd used it smartly by coming to a former teacher to help him navigate acquiring a part-time job. And yet, if he needed help with *this* endeavor, then getting his mother services would seem daunting.

Luckily, an idea popped into my head. We headed to the front office to speak with Delia Ortega, the campus's dropout prevention specialist and a good friend. Delia, also born outside the United States, had lost a mother to mental illness. My mind kept spinning. A while back, Delia happened to mention her weekend job at HEB, a local grocery store that employed a large number of high school students.

I couldn't have planned better what transpired next. There were no phone or administrative interruptions, which afforded Delia time to visit with us. She listened intently and asked few questions. Then, in her classy black high heels, she darted to the file cabinets. "I'm listening, *mi'jo*. Continue," she said. Back at her desk, she opened the file and began taking notes. When Noé paused longer than usual—he'd paused a lot—she leaned forward and offered a perfect solution. It was as if she'd read my mind. "What about HEB? They hire students like you all the time. Can you read Spanish?"

"Yes," Noé answered.

"And English?" Delia pressed.

He faltered. "A little."

"Good. Then you could start by stocking fruits and vegetables. You'd have to work early in the morning or late at night. Is that okay?"

"Okay, but . . ."

"But what? What's worrying you, *mi'jo*?" Delia questioned, arranging the papers in his folder. She nodded, seeming to know what he would say next.

"I don't have a social security number."

"Don't worry about that. It's not a problem," she assured him. "I work at HEB every Saturday morning, the one on Riverside. Do you know which HEB I'm talking about?"

"The one by Parker Road?"

"Exactly. Come on Saturday between nine and ten

o'clock. The manager will be there, and I'll introduce you to him." She handed him her card with her name and office number. He read it then stowed it in his wallet. She stood up, signaling she was out of time.

Noé rose, meekly extending his hand. "Thank you, Miss," he mumbled.

"*De nada*. See you Saturday," Delia said matter-of-factly.

I thought about stopping Noé on his way out and having him review the plans. Just to be certain he had the time and place right. Miscommunications happened. Instead, I watched his trim frame pass by the front counter, through the main door to the courtyard, and out of sight.

It wasn't until the following week that I had a chance to speak with Delia. I asked her as nonchalantly as I could about Noé. He'd never showed up at HEB.

"Maybe he came late," I suggested, hoping she'd somehow missed him. Or that he'd met with the manager without her.

"No, Miss. I don't think so. I was there all day." Sensing my dismay, she shook her head. "You know, these things happen. If he's a smart boy—and he seemed to be—he'll find his way. You can only do so much." She shrugged and turned to answer the phone. Maybe she herself had been let down too many times by too many troubled teenagers.

I had a class to teach and copies to run off. My busyness didn't allow much room for disappointment to sink in. But there's no denying the fact that it's disheartening when you feel you've provided someone with an opportunity, especially a fortuitous one, and they fail to take advantage of it.

Driving home that afternoon, I reminded myself that I couldn't walk in another person's shoes. Who knows what obstacles Noé had faced that Saturday? I pegged his mother as the culprit. I decided she'd had an episode and needed to be taken to the emergency room. Or else she didn't believe him about HEB and had forbidden him from leaving the house. Or maybe Noé had forgotten. Or overslept. Unlikely, either of those last two. But, granted, conceivable.

I took one final action—a phone call to the high school counselors and ESL teachers to apprise them of Noé's home situation. But he was soon to be eighteen, a legal adult, past the age when I could call Child Protective Services about him.

Where Noé is in life now, I have no idea. The day I watched him walk out the front office was the last time I saw him. I regret not having done more, like finding him at the high school and driving him to HEB to help arrange an interview, or researching solutions for his mother's care. This is a teacher's dilemma—which battles to fight, which fires to put out. My memory of Noé, though, is a gift. It was students like him, in situations like his, that sustained and nudged me toward my commitment to remain in the field.

Marking *Territorio*

"I think every school in America should have a Bring Your Dog to School Day." Allie, the daughter of my friend Sarah, proposed this from the back seat of Sarah's Suburu. The station wagon was loaded with two adults (Sarah and me), two kids (Allie and my son Jonas), four bikes, and two dogs. We were headed for any scenic country road that grabbed our fancy. I could have sworn I saw, from the corner of my eye, our dog Simon and their dog Chip—best canine buddies— take a break from panting and drooling to grin ear to ear at Allie's pronouncement.

"That would be so awesome. So fun." Allie was almost whining, she wanted so badly for her idea to come to fruition.

How ingenious! I thought. Allie, an honest-to-goodness dog-lover, was onto something.

My mind wandered to the incident she'd reported to me a few weeks earlier—the one about Simon managing to sneak onto the school bus. He'd followed her to the bus stop and waited at her feet as she stroked his coat and irresistibly soft ears. "I checked to make sure he didn't follow me onto the bus," she'd told me. "I kept looking out the window, and I could see him sitting on the ground, his tail swishing the dirt on the sidewalk, his pink tongue hanging out of his mouth like it always does. But he must've climbed the steps right before the driver closed the doors." It was true. Simon, the Harry Houdini of dogs, had somehow slithered on board seconds before the bus took off. Of course, he made it only a few yards before the bus lurched to a stop and the driver shooed him off. "Everybody was laughing so hard," Allie had said, chuckling.

When I asked her what Simon did then, she'd replied, "Just pranced toward your house, all in a huff."

Now, as we drove through the countryside, my teacher brain churned with a bright new idea. Simon would no doubt enjoy the classroom, full of bustling energy and kids doting over him. He went to great lengths not to be alone; yet, unfortunately, that was how he spent the majority of the work week.

Happening upon a farm-to-market road—a few cattle guards, occasional wildlife sightings, and minimal traffic— we parked and started out on our bikes. Simon and Chip, tails straight up, ran ahead and sniffed for lizards and rabbits in the brush. I watched as my dog, a smaller-than-average black Labrador, clearly kept to the side of the road, carving paths away from it, almost never toward it. As I often did, I happily observed his impressive natural intelligence . . . and that was when my vision, inspired by Allie's pronouncement, really took shape: Simon *could* take a seat at a table in my portable.

A rule follower (except for sneaking onto school buses), Simon rarely barked, never jumped on people, and preened himself constantly. I imagined using my dog as a model for good discipline. Didn't he sit when he heard "Sit!"? Didn't he lift a paw when he heard "Shake!"? And didn't he stay put when he heard "Wait!"? Maybe my students would adopt such compliant behavior—and oh! how much easier my job would be.

A pickup truck with a thunderous motor approached

from behind. As if somehow tied in to my daydreaming, my son commanded, "Simon, siiiiiiide." Allie did likewise. "Chip, grass." Simon immediately plunked his body down along the border of weeds at the edge of the asphalt. Chip, dazed by the oncoming loud noise and the panic in Allie's voice, froze.

A done deal. I could foresee no problem with taking obedient Simon for a classroom visit in the near future.

Before my students ever met Simon, they knew some of his history. I'd showed them photos and told them simple stories starring my dog. Then, the day before they saw him for the first time, an incident personally—maybe even emotionally—connected him to them.

Early that morning I'd put Simon in the backyard of a friend and fellow teacher. Sonia Cruz's house was close enough to the school that during my lunch period I could drive there, walk Simon, and get back in time for my first afternoon class. Yet my plan to give him a break from spending long days alone at home hadn't included another canine Harry Houdini act.

When I got to Sonia's house, leash in hand, the yard was empty. I drove around in the vicinity, calling his name, but no black Lab appeared. Totally distressed and with only minutes to spare, I raced back to my portable. Students filed into the room in their usual rambunctious fashion, having just enjoyed forty minutes of free time and lunch in the cafeteria. Boys punched and tripped each other. Girls reached behind a friend to pull a ponytail, then looked away to feign innocence. Grief-stricken, I simply sat and waited for everyone's attention—none of the usual shushing or clapping to quieten them. Slowly, kid by kid, the playfulness and chatter subsided. Then the nudging elbows, the sideways glances, and the fingers pointing at me trickled to a halt as well.

María broke the awkward silence. "Ms. Smith, something the matter?"

"Yes, I'm very sad," I murmured. "My dog is gone. He ran away. *Mi perro se fue.*"

"Simon? You puppy black?" Ernesto asked incredulously, pronouncing "Simon" as *See-MON* and "puppy" as *POO-pee*. The photos he'd seen had obviously made an impression.

I nodded. More silence.

Taking advantage of their anguish, I decided to explain. (It would be a great opportunity for the class to practice listening.) "I brought Simon to Ms. Cruz's house early this morning because her house is close to the school. My house is far away. I put Simon in Ms. Cruz's backyard so I could visit him during lunch. But when I went back to Ms. Cruz's house, Simon was not there. He jumped the fence."

Again María, eyes wide as a four-lane road: "But, Miss, we can go and look now for you dog. Just walking."

I was touched by her generosity—really, all of the kids' compassion was so unexpected—but I shook my head. "Oh, María, that's a nice idea. But we can't walk to Ms. Cruz's house. It's too far. And I already looked for Simon. I drove my car around the neighborhood. I looked in yards and streets."

"But maybe we can shout '*See-MON*' and he run back," suggested Simon's biggest fan, Ernesto. "Like this," he added, cupping his hands around his mouth and demonstrating.

"Maybe Simon will go back to Ms. Cruz's house when he gets hungry," I said. "He's a smart dog. And he's careful about cars."

With a heavy heart, I prompted the kids to take out their pencils and journals. They dutifully trudged to the journal trays, their backpacks, and the pencil sharpener.

Then the phone rang. As if in the middle of a game

of Freeze Tag, the kids—some standing, others sitting, some reaching, others bending—went motionless and stared at my desk phone.

"Ms. Smith's classroom," I answered, breathless. I listened, not bothering to sit down, mouthing "oh my God" as the woman on the other end delivered each piece of good news. She worked at the city animal shelter where I'd adopted Simon, and the gist of her report was that someone had dropped him off minutes ago. Thank goodness I'd purchased an identification chip when I adopted him and so she knew who to contact.

I assured the woman I'd pick up my dog right after school then thanked her over and over. Just before hanging up, she warned me, "Next time he shows up here, we'll have to put him down. He's a repeat."

I shared all this, except for the last dire fact, with my students. A great roar went up. Ernesto literally jumped for joy, tossing his journal ceiling-ward. It spun like a sideways top, landing precisely at his place at the table. We gasped in unison at the near impossibility of this feat, sensing that it somehow confirmed Simon's being located as a miracle as well. And on that happy afternoon I decided my dog would visit my classes the next day. After all, the kids deserved confirmation of his condition.

Nineteen hours later, Simon and I were outside the portable, waiting to greet my first class. While in wait, he lifted his leg several times to "relieve" himself on the cement gym wall opposite the ramp ending at the portable's door. Then he plopped down in its shadow on the rough pavement, crossing his front paws as usual. Once the kids turned the corner, they yelped and sprinted to the ramp as if in a relay race. Luckily, the commotion didn't scare Simon. He remained in position, with some added tail-wagging and a pointed nose sniffing in the direction of the onslaught. The scene played out like the opening sequence of a modern-day *Lassie* TV show.

The fifteen or so kids gathered around Simon, all except Soe Lin and Thida, both Burmese. They hung back, holding a seemingly pleasant conversation. Yet they repeatedly glanced at Simon to keep tabs on his whereabouts. And it was obvious from how they'd positioned their bodies—leaning on a backpack pressed against the gym wall, one leg bent at a right angle—that they were ready to spring if my dog got too close.

Simon quickly tired of the "oohs" and "ahhs," stood up, and walked to the door. One student directed the others' attention toward him. "*Miren.* The *POO-pee* want go to school."

"*See-MON* is a *POO-pee* very good," another chimed in.

We followed Simon into the portable, where he promptly beelined it to the favored yellow beanbag in a front corner of the room. Another round of laughter. "And *See-MON* a dog smart," Miguel Ángel declared.

Enough time had been taken up that I allowed the class to skip the daily warm-up and go straight to the computers. The kids knew to leave the overhead fluorescent lights off since the computers generated enough light. They appreciated the calming effect of a slightly darkened room. So did Simon. He promptly went to sleep on his already claimed beanbag. With his black coat difficult to make out in the unlit room, he slowly faded from view and consciousness as everyone became mesmerized by the computer screens.

So far, so good, I thought. Simon fit right in, not too much of a distraction. Yet no sooner had I relaxed than the principal walked in. He proceeded to the far side of the room, where the kids worked. I prayed that Simon would go unnoticed, but I'd forgotten about his tail-wagging habit. Just as the principal passed near the beanbag, a loud thumping on vinyl rose from the dimly lit corner. The principal stopped in his tracks. He took in Simon. Then his gaze spanned the rest of the room, the line of kids quietly typing, and finally me at my desk. I shrugged, caught with my hands in the cookie jar. Without a word, he did an about-face and left, shaking his head before the door shut behind him.

Simon visited my classroom only one other time—to the dismay of most students, even the Burmese, who would periodically ask about him. "You still have Simon, the happy dog?" Simon at home (and far from the school) provided a sense of relief, although a small part of them wished that weren't the case.

During that second and last visit, my students and I walked eight blocks to the public library. They'd filled out library card applications; now they needed to be issued the cards and practice using them. The route there was a straight shot with one dangerous intersection. Along the way, small houses, some in wild landscaping, some adorned with creative and at times outrageous yard art, offered much to look at. It was a perfect spring morning: flowers, birds, and, of course, endless new smells (good and bad) for Simon.

What amazed me on this library field trip was how a dog like Simon—or maybe, not to be partial, any dog— sparked the inner child in even the roughest of my bunch. Omar, the wanna-be gangster who incessantly teased kids displaying the slightest degree of enthusiasm toward me or any activity that hinted of playfulness, insisted on being first in line to hold Simon's leash. It was Omar who got several turns holding it (much to the chagrin of Miguel Ángel, who got one turn fewer). And it was Omar who lovingly waited with Simon outside the library.

No one noticed Omar's behavior change, or the fact that six-foot-tall Federico jogged a whole city block in his high-tops and falling-from-the-waist jeans, pulled by Simon—a new form of joy riding. No one noticed because their main preoccupation had been the number of times my dog urinated from the campus to the library. Thirty-eight, to be exact.

"Dang, Miss. Why *See-MON* pee so much times?" Miguel Ángel asked.

"He's marking his territory," I answered.

"What that mean—marking *territorio*?"

"He's letting all the dogs in the neighborhood know he was here. It's kind of like"—I started singing—*"This land is your land, and this land is my land . . ."*

"Oh. *See-MON* like a *inmigrante* to here. To Texas. And the other dogs need share the *territorio* and be friends to *See-MON.*"

"You got it, Miguel Ángel," I said, wishing it could be that simple.

Vanished

Graphic organizers are great pre-writing tools. One type, the Venn diagram, helps students organize ideas when they're asked to write a compare and contrast essay. The overlapping section in the middle of the Venn diagram lists characteristics that two subjects have in common, while the two outer sections display the differences between the subjects.

I didn't have to write an essay comparing and contrasting my students Dulce and Beatriz, of course. But if I had, here's what my Venn diagram would have looked like:

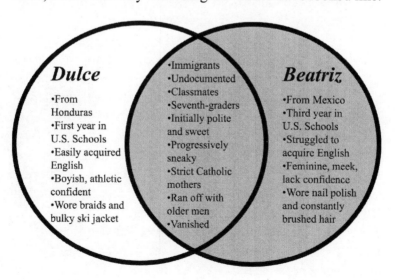

Dulce's mother sat at an empty table, her back erect. Dressed in jeans and a navy-blue jacket, hands folded in front of her, she stared straight ahead at her daughter. Dulce giggled and chatted with friends at the whiteboard. They played round after round of Tic-tac-toe. Immersed in the fun, Dulce didn't turn around even once to look at or speak to her mother, who remained somber, with Dulce her sole focus and reason for being there.

The bell sounded and Dulce crowded out the door with the rest of the kids. The mother continued to watch her through the portable window. Dulce headed in the direction of her first class of the day. One had to trust that that was where she was going. She dropped out of sight once she'd turned the corner. The mother slowly got up, pushed in the chair, and quietly walked to my desk to thank me. Her serious, genuine nature saddened me. Her life saddened me. Before leaving, she quietly voiced the same reminder she did every morning she was there, that her husband would pick Dulce up after school at three-thirty sharp. Her worried face searched my own, beseeching me for ideas as to what else could be done for her daughter. Then she rushed off to her cleaning job in a downtown hotel, hoping her marginally late arrival didn't jeopardize her employment.

Dulce had been under parental surveillance since her first disappearance. The same as for many immigrant parents, the natural inclination of Dulce's mother and father was to maintain a low profile, even in the school community. But this proved problematic when faced with the possibility of their child becoming a runaway.

When Dulce was returned to them after having been missing for two weeks, they reinstated her and requested to meet with the guidance office. The counselors emailed Dulce's seven teachers, instructing them to notify the attendance office immediately if Dulce Zelaya didn't show up to class. But Dulce's face had yet to become a familiar one since she was relatively new and had already been absent those two weeks of her disappearance. And her teachers had a hundred-plus other students. The attendance alert, although not futile, offered a weak safeguard.

At thirteen, Dulce, whether in the classroom, the cafeteria, the gym, or apparently at home, needed to be occupied. She inhaled knowledge at a pace always one step ahead of her peers. Metaphorically speaking, she would complete the jigsaw puzzle before anyone else had lifted a single piece. If her brain became idle, her body shifted into nonstop motion.

Here's an example. One morning, as students worked in their reading groups, I circulated to observe progress and offer support. I intended to spend several minutes with each foursome, plunking myself down in a nearby student desk. Locating text evidence to support an answer choice within a two-page passage wasn't a popular skill to practice.

"How do you know the dog is a smart mother?" I pressed the first group. Two students predictably pointed to the title of the passage: "A Good Mother."

"Yes, the title says 'good.' But 'smart' isn't the same as 'good.' What in the story does the mother do that tells you she's *smart*?" My question signaled the kids to reread the text. They bent their heads over the pages and dragged their pencils excruciatingly slowly along the lines of text. In my left field of vision, Dulce's hand quickly shot up.

"I know. I know," she announced breathlessly from the neighboring group. Dulce would be getting my attention soon enough, but now she was waving her hand impatiently.

Leaving the first group to search on their own, I repositioned my desk to face Dulce and her three partners. Dulce's appearance changed little from day to day: a ski jacket that stayed zipped, two thick braids barely touching her shoulders, her only jewelry a cross hanging from a delicate neck chain. She greeted me with a generous smile, tapping my shoulder to get me to check her paper first. Too quick for the group, frustrated by the others' ambivalence, she'd worked on her own. I intended only to skim the paper to satisfy her need for recognition. Surely this would take only seconds, since she couldn't possibly have finished the exercise in less than ten minutes. Surprisingly, though, not only did she have all four answers correct; she'd also highlighted in pink the sentences from the passage that supported her answer choices.

"Miss, is right. Right? So I can bring attendance to the office?" she asked. Like a sly fox, Dulce would soon be up to mischief if I didn't provide a diversion. Since she had no interest in peer tutoring, I sent her to a counselor who I knew was trying to meet a deadline. He could use a quick assistant to alphabetize files.

I imagine that life in Texas had proven to be a drastic change for an extrovert like Dulce. Raised by her grandmother in a Honduran village, surrounded by extended family and neighbors, she now found herself confined to a drab apartment complex and living with relative strangers—her parents. They'd left Dulce in Honduras at the age of six and risked their lives to enter the United States. Then they worked incredibly hard to save enough money to send for her. Seven years later, Dulce rejoined her parents. She was thirteen and barely knew them.

Her mother and father still worked long hours. They'd also dedicated themselves to their Pentecostal church. Dulce spent her non-school time either attending church services or watching TV alone in her apartment, shut off from the community. Her social circle dramatically reduced, she felt trapped. Naturally her adolescent spirit was going to resist.

I began to hear rumors based on the counseling sessions with Dulce and her parents: Dulce being made to kneel on rice, a strict form of punishment; her mother entering the country by hiding in the space for the spare wheel of a huge truck; Dulce, during her disappearance, staying with an older man in exchange for taking care of his young children. (She complained of not having enough to eat during that time yet elected to be hungry rather than reunite with her parents.)

I tried to figure out Dulce and other immigrant young people not fully entrenched in American culture. Could it be that traces of the iconic rebellious American teenager image—the unruly behavior, the drugs and promiscuity—still lingered, appealing to and influencing them? That my students sensed they were missing out on something exciting? If so, this perception, coupled with their undocumented parents' zealous supervision stemming from fear of the law and of attention brought to their families, might increase these students' feelings of isolation.

Even in the general population, creating close family ties has become increasingly challenging. People of all ages stay plugged in to their electronic devices. In many cases, both parents work outside the home. Their children, involved in after-school and weekend activities, also spend more time away from home. Family gatherings may be less common because relatives are more likely to be scattered.

Other aspects of being immigrants further complicate family relationships. The parents' jobs—often in service industries, which means weekend hours, night shifts, and working on holidays—impinge on family time. What's more, conflicts in families are often heightened since they're rooted not only in generational issues but also cultural issues. Young people more easily assimilate, and then their parents quite possibly feel left behind, disappointed, even threatened.

Yet I believe that the overriding factor for immigrant families not staying connected is the extended period of geographic separation during a child's formative years. The fact that Dulce hadn't seen her parents for so long was typical for the students I taught. Dulce's parents hadn't raised her. She continually referred to and wrote about her grandmother, not her parents.

The adage "One cannot demand respect; one must earn it" rang true. Dulce's parents hadn't had enough time to gain her respect. Their daughter's allegiance lay with her grandmother.

I moved from Dulce's group to Beatriz's. Dulce and Beatriz were classmates but never friends—opposites in many ways, yet destined for the same fate. Dulce sought the thrill of adventure to escape boredom; Beatriz yearned for love and attention. Dulce had to be redirected; Beatriz almost always needed prompting.

Beatriz came to my classroom every day with her waist-length hair wet and reeking of shampoo. Once it dried, she spent the remainder of the class brushing it. She often wore tight hip-hugger jeans, cinched with a wide, white patent-leather belt, and a yellow T-shirt emblazoned with "Viva México." This morning, in typical fashion, Beatriz, obsessed with the smoothness of her hair, had yet to glance at the passage the other students were reading. When I asked her why she hadn't started, she shrugged and giggled. She twisted to one side of her seat and then the other like a Slinky toy. At a loss as to what to do next, she stretched her arms in front of her, spreading all ten fingers to inspect her nail job.

Despite having attended American schools since fifth grade, Beatriz knew little English—less than Dulce, who had been in the United States only four months. Beatriz blurted out English words with a laugh, covering her mouth and looking away. She cracked up whenever her friends spoke English, like it was a language she'd never heard before. She considered anything American as somehow silly. She pointed to pictures of hairstyles or outfits in fashion magazines and snickered. Certain popular music she found hilarious, and her head and shoulders shook with disdain as she listened. She appeared serious and engaged only

122

when the subject involved her culture: a song or poem in Spanish, a story with Mexican characters, a fleeting image of a famous Mexican actor. Then she would beam with pride. Because I sensed her hackles rise whenever I got close, I stayed mindful of her personal space. I was another "gringa" she didn't trust.

One day Beatriz surprised me by asking if she could make up some work after school. Arriving seconds after the last bell, she took her assigned seat even though we were alone in the classroom. I sat at my desk catching up on phone calls.

"Do you have your work?" I whispered, covering the mouthpiece. She nodded and in slow motion took a paper from her backpack and centered it on the desk. Next, she moseyed over to the pencil sharpener and made three attempts to perfect the pencil's point, each time bringing it to her lips to gently blow away the shavings. Then she slid back into the seat, put one foot up on it, and wrapped her arms around the bent leg.

"Let me know if you need my help," I offered and continued my phone conversation. From time to time I glanced discreetly in her direction. She stared out the window when she heard students passing by. I wanted her to show some initiative, to explain what she needed help with. I hung up and started entering grades into the computer.

The next time I looked up, Beatriz was standing at my desk. She'd moved so quietly I hadn't heard her.

"Miss," she said sweetly, peering down with large Powerpuff Girls eyes. "Can I use your phone?"

"Yes," I replied, disappointed by her request. She needed to arrange a ride home.

She dialed in an oddly jerky way. Then I remembered that her hands often trembled, which I'd attributed to shyness and a lack of confidence.

"Primero necesitas marcar el nueve." My instructions to dial a nine first for an outside number seemed

to add to her anxiety. She fumbled with the phone, not waiting long enough for a dial tone. Finally, I dialed for her.

After writing the following day's agenda on the board and tidying up the room, I returned to my desk. Still on the phone, Beatriz had curled up in a chair. Twisting the phone cord around her fingers and smiling coyly, she tossed her head back and laughed. Clearly, she was not discussing a way to get home.

"Beatriz," I called from the door, "I'll be right back." Engrossed in her conversation, she didn't hear me. I raced to the counselor's office, hoping he hadn't left for the day. My students loved Mr. Keaton. He made them laugh in his eloquently spoken Spanish.

I was in luck. The counselor was still there, and when I said I urgently needed him to check on a student in my classroom, he dropped what he was doing.

On the way, I asked, "Do you know Beatriz Martinez?"

"Not by name, but probably by face," he replied.

"I think something's up with her. She came in after school supposedly for tutoring. But she asked to borrow the classroom phone, and she's been talking to someone for a while. I'm guessing it's a boyfriend she's been forbidden to have any contact with."

In his typical jocular fashion, he took a pencil and small notepad from his shirt pocket, hunched himself over as if adjusting an overcoat, and announced, "Columbo to the rescue."

Wanting to give Beatriz and him privacy, I went to the workroom and made copies for the next day's lessons. When I returned, Beatriz had gone. But Mr. Keaton had performed admirable detective work. She'd confessed that, yes, she was talking to a boy on the phone. Initially she told the counselor the boy was her cousin, then later admitted it was a twenty-year-old boyfriend her mother didn't approve of. "Well, of course your mother wouldn't," Mr. Keaton said he'd told her. Beatriz, a thirteen-year-old, had no business dating a guy seven years older. The counselor and I parted, agreeing to monitor Beatriz closely.

Days later, Mr. Keaton and a female colleague stopped by my classroom on their way to a home visit with Beatriz and her mother. Pacing back and forth, he described an upsetting phone call from Beatriz. Her mother was keeping her home from school because Beatriz had been "caught" with the boyfriend and her mother refused to let her leave the apartment. Then he came to the delicate part: her mother had examined Beatriz herself to determine if she remained a virgin.

Since I now knew more of Beatriz's story—and she knew that I knew—I expected her attitude to be different when she returned to school, the tension between us to be somewhat diminished. But neither one happened. It was then that I started to understand the power and the built-up layers of complicated family dynamics. Before long, Beatriz was gone for good, reported as a runaway.

On the heels of Beatriz's disappearance, Dulce also became an official runaway for the second time. Her parents' plan, inevitably, had failed. Dulce slipped from view during the school day, hours before her father arrived to pick her up. Just a week earlier, one of my colleagues had taken the thirteen-year-old to go trick-or-treating, and now she was on the run with an older man.

After Dulce's disappearance, in my head I composed a list of questions I'd ask her if given the opportunity.

- Did you run away with the same man?
- And if so, are you hungry?
- Did you yearn for the romance and adventure that you see in movies and on social media?
- Won't you miss your friends and teachers?
- Did you feel so stifled by your parents and yo·
here that you had to make such a drastic move?

- Do you ever think of how much your parents sacrificed for seven years to provide you with a brighter future?
- Is this man and the life he's providing you worth everything else?
- Maybe you've ended up back in Honduras? With your grandmother? Yes, Dulce, maybe your escape was your way of ultimately returning.

Presumed Invulnerable

"¿En-ti-en-des?" Sylvie carefully enunciated the word to Itzel, her Spanish-speaking classmate seated across the aisle. Itzel looked back and forth from her textbook to my face a few times. Next, Sylvie bent over Itzel's desk, as a teacher might, resting one arm on the back of the chair and the other on the desk.

"¿No me entiendes?" she asked, a smile stretched wide, almost reaching the braids that bordered her dimpled cheeks. The two girls fell out laughing. Sylvie didn't actually speak Spanish, and of course Itzel knew this. Sylvie was imitating me.

My ESL colleague loved to brag about Sylvie: she entered sixth grade with three languages under her belt—French and two African languages—and left middle school with five, having added English and, to an impressive level, Spanish.

Sylvie learned Spanish almost accidentally. My colleague and I bore the brunt of the responsibility (or blame) for this. Since most of our students spoke Spanish exclusively, we resorted to it in a pinch, and many situations warranted a pinch. Our daily deviating to Spanish unfortunately sometimes frustrated the speakers of other languages in our classrooms. But not Sylvie. She echoed phrases and tones like the recording device that, with a push of a button, instantly plays back whatever was just said.

For sure, Sylvie had the Burmese students fooled. Once when I requested a student's assistance to interpret for a Spanish-speaking parent waiting outside the classroom, Soe Lin said, "Sylvie can do it."

"Sylvie doesn't speak Spanish," I replied a little curtly, not taking him seriously.

"What?" Soe Lin looked astonished. "No? She not from Honduras?"

"What?" I said, my turn to be astonished. "Sylvie is from a country in Africa where people speak French."

Soe Lin's jaw dropped and his eyebrows formed a *V*. He hung his head, shamed that Sylvie had managed to dupe him as she'd done in other matters.

"He-he-he, Soe Lin. You believe me," Sylvie ribbed, then burst into her usual round of giggles.

At the ripe age of thirteen Sylvie still enjoyed a round of hide-and-seek during recess or a sprinting race on the track behind the portable. She exuded energy, fun, and a propensity for teasing that seldom provoked others. Befriending students from Burma to Mexico, Honduras to China, she had a knack for drawing people together. In retrospect, I should have channeled her skills and encouraged her to form an international student club.

Although very attuned to languages, Sylvie, consciously or not, retained her French accent when she spoke English. Like Zsa Zsa Gabor in the 1960s TV sitcom *Green Acres*, Sylvie's *s* sounded more like a *z* and her *h* had excessive air flow.

"C'mon, don't be zad," she consoled a despondent Sandra one morning. "Be *hh*-appy." Sandra rebuffed Sylvie's concern, turning her head away and laying it on bent arms. She intermittently raised her head to wipe away tears. Not giving up, Sylvie arched her body over Sandra's back to meet her downcast gaze. Then she whispered in

Sandra's exposed ear. The hands she'd placed on either side of her mouth muffled her speech, and her laughter further suppressed the message. (Sylvie usually found hilarious whatever she'd said.) Slowly Sandra succumbed, and by the time Sylvie tickled her sides she had the giggles as well as hiccups.

Not only was Sylvie always at the ready to run an errand, play a game, act and sing in front of a camera, apologize for a mishap, or egg on anyone who needed it; she also dedicated herself to academics. She won second place in the annual ESL spelling bee, and in the four language domains—listening, speaking, reading, and writing—she eventually earned the highest rating, "advanced high," in all but reading. Sylvie's rapid accomplishments led me to assume a correlation between having a talent for acting and excelling at language acquisition—that the passion and ability to recreate a personality or voice facilitates language learning.

Sylvie seemed so remarkable in attitude and intelligence that I presumed her to be invulnerable. I recognized my mistake one morning in November when I unwittingly asked her to show her mother the way to the front office.

I was expecting Sylvie's mother to arrive at the school before the first bell. As our only parent representative on the school's LPAC (Language Proficiency Assessment Committee), a volunteer role mandated by the Texas Education Agency, she was coming to attend the required monthly meeting. Ordinarily the principal and I conducted this meeting during the latter part of the afternoon in a back office. Yet this particular meeting had been scheduled for 8:30 a.m. in the front office.

As usual, Sylvie's mother was punctual—no easy feat for a person dependent on public transportation. Uncertain where to report, she'd decided to meet me in my portable, a familiar location since it was Sylvie's ESL classroom and one that provided easy access from the street. A student opened the door, and in stepped Sylvie's mother, adorned in her elaborate Congolese garb: a long lavender and yellow batik wraparound dress and matching headdress. Sylvie, having arrived a few minutes earlier, continued to gab with her friends, giving no sign that she'd noticed her mother's entrance.

The mother nodded to me and took the first available seat. As I scurried to prepare for the substitute about to show up, I wondered why Sylvie and her mom had arrived separately, one on the city bus and the other on the school bus. Sylvie had a city bus pass. They could have come together. Feeling awkward about the mother having to endure Sylvie's aloofness, I suggested she go ahead to the meeting location. "Do you know how to get to the office from here?" I asked. She shook her head, and her bright smile turned to a frown. The campus, over 150 years old (hence, several add-ons), was notorious for the topsy-turvy arrangement of its buildings.

Without hesitating, I approached her daughter. "Sylvie, take your mom to the front office."

She froze at the blackboard, where she was writing her name in large cursive letters. "Okay, Miss," a very different Sylvie responded, keeping her back to me. Then, as she made her way to the door, she did something I'd never seen. *She rolled her eyes! Sylvie rolled her eyes!* She stood erect while her mother gathered belongings.

"Tell Ms. Simms I'll be there soon," I directed.

"All right," Sylvie replied in her new subdued voice.

How dare she treat her mother like this, I thought. From the window I watched them leave, Sylvie walking five yards ahead and gaining. Her mother traipsed behind, a colorful bird among a flock of gray pigeons. On this day her headdress loomed extra tall.

Suddenly it dawned on me exactly what Sylvie was about to experience: a journey that was never smooth-sailing for anyone. Five minutes until the morning bell, the entire student body continued to converge on the central courtyard—on Sylvie and her mother's exact route to the office. Even if it wasn't the whole school, it would feel like that to Sylvie. She found herself parading through passels of students, her mother in tow and clad in her traditional attire. If it had been Martin Luther King Day or any day in February (Black History Month), Sylvie's mother wouldn't have seemed out of the ordinary. But it was neither. It was a routine Friday in April. For many middle-schoolers, a parent showing up on school grounds caused shame and suffering—even worse when the parent shared their physical space. But to have the parent also stand out, either by behavior or appearance, was a young teen's worst nightmare.

In my mind I traced the various clusters the pair would likely confront on their way to the office. The first and most fearsome was the seventh-grade football players, a group of gangling, rambunctious males who spent their before-school minutes poking fun at each other and at anyone passing by who caught their attention. I always prayed to make it by their lineup without one of them pushing another into me.

Next, Sylvie and her mother would zigzag through two factions of sixth-grade girls who usually were engaged in a shouting match over some boy. In switching girlfriends, the boy in question might have relinquished his loyalty to one group in order to join the ranks of the other. The girls, drenched in perfume and bling, wore hot pink T-shirts displaying an array of gold-glittered assertive slogans. From their small O-shaped mouths lathered in pink lipstick, obscenities were being spewed, which caused passersby to cringe and consider turning around and retreating. Thankfully, Sylvie's mom remained oblivious to the language, although their pitch alone was deafening. One benefit: the girls, busy eyeing and sizing up each other, allowed the passersby to proceed largely unnoticed.

Beyond this spectacle, Sylvie and her mother would

encounter the long, sprawled-out legs and formidably positioned handbags and backpacks of the eighth-grade girls from the magnet school. They created a maze of jacks games and sidewalk chalk diagrams. With a rainbow of hair colors—purple, pink, blue—they sat or lay in yoga positions on the hard cement, sharing art projects or engrossed in conversation about a teacher's injustice. Of all the groups, the magnet-school clique would be most likely to find Sylvie's mom "cool." They, at an early age, embraced diversity and multiculturalism. Imagining all this, I had a fleeting notion that cruising through a public school's courtyard ten minutes before the beginning bell offered a true glimpse into adolescent behavior in twenty-first-century America.

Once my sub arrived, I followed the same path as Sylvie and her mother had, keeping the chaos at arm's length, knowing there would be enough of it in the hours that lay ahead. The office overflowed with activity. Substitutes hurried to their assigned spots. Parents with questions or concerns for the office staff filled the straight-backed chairs along a wall. Kids returning from absences with medical notes or other excuses formed a line from the front desk to the back exit. The security guard seemed to have under control the one minor mishap of the morning: a fight between two female students that had started off-campus. No longer in combative mode, they sat face to face, looking away now and then in tearful jerks like little birds scouting for seeds. The guard attempted to contact their parents with the phone numbers the girls mumbled to him.

Sylvie and her mom had arrived apparently unscathed, but Sylvie maintained her measured distance. The mom joined the seated parents, while Sylvie leaned on the front counter, blending in with the returning students. I looked in the AP's (assistant principal's) office, a small room off the main office. Finding it empty, I stepped behind the counter to assist waiting students. Sylvie spotted me and subtly inched closer.

"Miss," she said softly after moving out of everyone's earshot, "can I go now, please?" Still refusing to look at me, she rearranged brochures lying on the counter.

"Yes, of course. Thank you," I answered as I signed a kid's reinstatement pass.

"You're welcome," Sylvie said in the sullen tone she'd used all morning. She dashed out the door without even a parting wave to her mother. I caved in to my disappointment. Sylvie didn't walk the fine line I thought she did. She'd taken one step too many in distancing herself from her culture and had hurt her mother in the process.

The bell sounded and Ms. Simms, the AP, rushed in from bus duty, looking as if she'd barely avoided a tornado. She politely held the door for the last exiting students. The place had cleared out of staff and lingering parents, so no one sidetracked her on the way to her office. She tossed her keys into a desk drawer, put down her walkie-talkie, and arranged hair that wind had forced out from under barrettes. I beckoned to Sylvie's mother to join us.

Ms. Simms and I adored Conny. (That was her first name, which we used to address her in the meetings.) Seemingly never unnerved or out of sorts, she beamed a contagious smile that revealed perfectly straight white teeth. Conny's beauty was timeless and healthy. I felt a heart-to-heart connection with her, just as Ms. Simms did, since all three of us were women of a similar age and mothers of adolescents. And if it weren't for the language barrier—Conny spoke French but very little English—we'd have been fast friends.

Ms. Simms handed me the list of new students we needed to discuss. I gave it to Conny as I explained what it was. *"La liste des nouveaux élèves."* In these meetings I would at times employ my college-learned French with her, never sure if it helped or hindered communication. Now, Conny nodded and reiterated what I'd said in more eloquent French.

Knowing that Ms. Simms needed to leave shortly for an administrators' meeting across town, I zipped through the information on the new arrivals. "Eladio, Francisco, and Yazmín. All from Mexico. All three scored a zero in English proficiency. So I placed them in my beginning ESL class."

"And how are they doing?" Ms. Simms asked. Before I could reply, a loud female voice thundered from the AP's walkie-talkie: "Ms. Simms, what's your twenty?"

The AP raised it to her mouth and firmly stated, "I'm in my office in an LPAC meeting and not to be disturbed."

"Ten-four," the voice blasted back, followed by loud static. Turning down the volume, Ms. Simms smiled and waited for my response.

"Well, Yazmín already has a ton of friends eager to help her with her work. And the two boys are brothers, so they have each other for support. The younger brother writes slowly and cautiously, but he might simply be anxious. Hard to tell. I think they'll be fine in a few weeks." I considered interpreting for Conny everything I'd said, but Ms. Simms already had her pen in hand. We passed the notes between us, each adding a signature, and the meeting was adjourned. As I watched Conny leave, I felt badly for her and for all the other LPAC parents over the years. They made a great effort to attend the monthly LPAC meetings, which often lasted a mere five minutes. So much production for such little substance. Like so many requirements in the bureaucracy of public education, rules became formalities.

I lingered in the privacy of the office, not eager to get my teaching day started. I remarked to Ms. Simms, a bit wistfully, "Sylvie hasn't been herself this morning. When I asked her to bring Conny to the office, she rolled her eyes at me and took off walking way ahead of her. I doubt she acknowledged or spoke to Conny the entire way. . . . Maybe Sylvie was embarrassed."

Ms. Simms, a stunning, self-assured Black woman who appreciated Sylvie's strong energy as much as I did, responded curtly, "She needs to get over it. She should be proud of her mother." Then the AP rushed off to her meeting.

As I stood alone in Ms. Simms's office, my disillusionment with Sylvie melted away. I realized that I didn't agree with the AP. Instead, I felt a budding empathy for Sylvie. *People acclimate at various speeds,* I reasoned. *Many of us never even have to acclimate.* Since I hadn't walked in Sylvie's shoes, to blame her seemed unfair.

My sensitivity to Sylvie's situation very possibly stemmed from my own childhood experiences. When I was in grade school in the mid-1960s, my (white) family moved from New England to a primarily Black community on Chicago's South Side. I soon identified with Black culture. I yearned for an afro, despising my long, wavy, unruly brown hair. I adored Diana Ross and other Motown performers and spurned the Beatles and the Beach Boys. I felt ashamed of the broken-down Chrysler my parents drove, inherited from my grandparents, while our neighbors and friends drove fashionable, well-taken-care-of cars. I desperately wanted to be the same as the people around us.

The middle-school years are still part of a complex stage in life: during this time children begin to define themselves. Layer that with simultaneously assimilating into another culture—and the path to self-discovery becomes even more involved and ambiguous. From an American standpoint, Sylvie had behaved like a typical thirteen-year-old in that she dreaded escorting her mother through those passels of students. And yet we educators who expect young teens to embrace their diversity in the company of large groups of their peers are misguided.

Many adults believe in the benefits that a rich diversity provides. We teach children to take pride in their unique qualities and heritage. We encourage children to show them off, not squash them. Yet we have to consider their maturity levels. Sylvie's mother intrigued Ms. Simms and me. She came from an African country, had a French accent, and wore beautiful clothes. Yes, Ms. Simms and I were curious about Conny's life experiences—so decidedly different from our own. *But Ms. Simms and I weren't thirteen.*

That said, in my classroom I'd seize opportunities that arose when students seemed willing to share something about their heritage with classmates. For instance, one afternoon I noticed Thida scribbling in her notebook in Burmese and suggested she demonstrate her elaborate handwriting on the blackboard. With some prodding from all of us, she agreed. She astounded everyone with her ability to quickly produce the detailed, ornate script. The length of the words amazed them too. *Boy* in Burmese was four or five inches long:

ယောက်ျားလေး

Thida could easily do something the rest of us would probably never master. Her peers' fascination and delight resulted in a proud moment for Thida. And in that moment her sense of vulnerability lost ground while her self-esteem made great gains. Not only had she exposed her talents but also her culture—a strong part of her identity.

At times I intentionally created situations that might prompt students to share some aspect of their culture. Once, with two Iraqi students in mind I chose a text to read aloud about an ancient library that had been destroyed in Iraq. As I'd hoped, the story struck a chord. The Iraqi boys became animated and, beaming with pride, spoke at length about the magnificent libraries and museums in the country they'd had to abandon. They ventured into sensitive territory, describing personal experiences with war. Their classmates, despite the boys' broken English, listened quietly.

When students disclosed facts about their personal lives, and the information was heard and appreciated, memorable connections happened. Such connections, and cherished interactions, and students learning from each other . . . these things served as reminders to me of why I'd chosen to be an educator.

One other memory I have of Sylvie also hints at her underlying desire to become American as apple pie. It involved a name change. In the spring semester of her first year, I implemented an approach called Suggestopedia. The example of Suggestopedia I'd studied in graduate school involved students "adopting" a new identity—a pseudonym and a career—that they claimed exclusively while in their ESL classroom. The theory behind this method is that when language learners assume a different persona, they're more prone to perform, to be less inhibited, and, thus, to take risks with language. The more that students risk, the faster they acquire the language. I thought this strategy would work well with the class, particularly with Sylvie.

On their first day back from winter break, my students sat in a circle, looking with curiosity at the three lists I'd written on large poster paper and taped to the blackboard.

"We're going to do something different this semester," I explained. "This list here is of some American first names." I used my pointer as I spoke. "Let's read them together."

"Jennifer, Vanessa, Michael, Samuel, Charlie, Sarah . . ." the students recited in unison. I'd tried to include names (like Sarah) that appear in a variety of languages and countries.

Next, they recited the list of last names. "Brown, Johnson, Jackson, Smith, Jones, Baker, Summers . . ."

Finally, we went down the career list. "Mechanic, coach, teacher, chef, scientist, beautician, plumber, pharmacist, doctor, artist . . ."

Before I had a chance to direct students to pick a first and last name and a career, Sylvie waved both hands in the air. "Ooh, Miss," she interrupted, covering her mouth in her typical fashion so she wouldn't start laughing uncontrollably. "I want to be 'Ashley.' Please. 'Ashley.' I love that name."

"Let's draw numbers to see who gets to choose a name first," I cautioned. "Someone else might also want 'Ashley.' And we need to be fair." Sylvie scrunched up her face, making a pouty lip. But she'd already started tearing small pieces of paper to write numbers on.

As I'd anticipated, Sylvie's undying enthusiasm pressed reluctant learners forward, and all the students welcomed the idea of adopting a different identity in their ESL class. In the end, Sylvie got her way. She became "Ashley Baker, women's basketball coach." The actor in her could hardly contain her excitement.

"Listen carefully. The name you picked is what we're going to call you in this class for the rest of the year," I instructed.

"The rest of the year?" Sylvie repeated, eyes wide open. "Really? Oh my God. I'm Ashley Baker, everybody, and don't forget it."

"Yes, and don't forget to write your new names on your assignments instead of your real names," I warned, then suddenly felt anxious about the confusion the name changes might entail for me.

Sylvie, off to the races, was already writing the curviest *Ashley* she could muster.

Unfortunately, by February, the state-appointed month for the testing of ESL students, our game (so to speak) had lost its momentum. Students spent hours completing forms, filling in their official names, birthdates, school ID numbers, genders, ethnicities. They wrote individual letters in squares then darkened circles below the squares to match the letters. The tedious process seemed determined to confirm their real identities and stamp out any variation. The

138

exams continued ad nauseum: timed reading tests and the practice ones prior to them; writing narrative, descriptive, and expository samples. There was no time for fun. No time for creative learning. When the testing finally ended, my weary students looked forward to one thing only—spring break.

But Sylvie remained "Ashley Baker" for the rest of the school year. I have a sneaking suspicion that if she called me today, she'd say, "Miss Smith, this is Ashley. Ashley Baker. Remember me?" I imagine her cracking up, barely able to hold the phone. After a few seconds, she gets a hold of herself and admits in her beautiful French accent, "No, this is Sylvie. Remember?"

I actually did hear from Sylvie once via her cell phone. Sadly, she'd had to transfer to another middle school for eighth grade because her family moved. The location of their new apartment complex, though close to the one they'd left, put them inside a different school zone. A major disappointment for Sylvie, she shed lots of tears, as did all her friends. But she got over it quickly, I'm sure. Making new friends would never be a problem for her.

Sylvie's call came on a Friday evening in October. Intent on understanding a particular word in a recipe, she didn't mention her adopted identity of "Ashley Baker" at all. The previous summer Sylvie had participated in a sleepover camp I'd held at my house for a few days. Since I lived near a lake, the girls could swim, canoe, and go boating. On one of the mornings, I made them waffles for breakfast. Sylvie had never eaten waffles and fell in love with them. After emptying her plate, she asked where she could find a waffle iron like mine. That was in June. Now, having saved her money and bought one, she was calling me.

"Ms. Smith, what is *batter*? I look it up in the dictionary and it talk about baze-bowl or something like that." Here was a teachable moment for words with multiple meanings, albeit over the phone. We shared a good laugh after I explained to her that *batter* not only referred to a player of a certain sport but also to the mixture for the waffles. "Oh my God. I am stupid," she said, giggling. I assured her she was far from stupid.

Once again, I recognized the fact that just because Sylvie giggled when she offhandedly called herself stupid didn't mean she was immune to self-doubt. Our immigrant students walk through obstacles in their early lives that may, in the long run, give them extra strength of character. Yet they're as vulnerable to fears of rejection and inadequacy as the rest of us.

Shattered

Holding our sides, gasping for breath, sliding off our seats, we laughed at every twist and turn of the mock ceremony being performed in the classroom. The traditional wedding march played from a cassette tape while students sat in chairs arranged in church-sanctuary formation. Yellow and pink crepe paper looped along the outer chairs of the two sections to demarcate the aisle, creating a festive atmosphere. Thuy, the pseudo bride, ambled down the aisle outfitted in a long white dress and a crown of flowers and giggling so hard she almost cried. Thuy joined the groom, Geovanny, the shortest boy in the class, who draped her arm in his. Geovanny somehow managed to keep a poker face the entire ceremony.

The student actors presented an unlikely pair. Thuy, a painfully shy eighth-grader from Vietnam, avoided attention at all costs. When she'd agreed to be the bride—something so out of character for her—students felt a mixture of disbelief and delight. The groom, on the other hand, a sixth-grader from El Salvador, was worthy of the class clown award. Part stuntman, part comedian, he had us in stitches each time he did a flip off his chair from a standing position and landed squarely on two feet, or imitated the school librarian's distinctive and annoying voice. Whenever a balled-up piece of paper sailed through the air from the back of the room into the wastebasket, it was a sure bet Geovanny had shot it. The girls fell secretly in love with him. The boys loved him because the girls loved him. I loved him because he kept the class entertained.

None of the male students had dared to volunteer for the groom's role, yet Geovanny had had no qualms. And his pretense of seriousness during the ceremony made it all the more hilarious. He put everyone at ease, allowing them to laugh at him and themselves. I knew I couldn't have pulled off the mini-drama without him.

The official name for the instructional strategy of the wedding ceremony is Realia. Teachers use *real* material—in this case, props, music, costumes—to engage students and enhance learning. Fun aside, the wedding ceremony incorporated specific learning objectives. Students practiced using the structures "will you" and "I will" in a relatable context. In preparation, I'd written a simplified version of the marriage vows. My students probably never forgot little Geovanny saying "I will" when the pretend minister asked him if he "will always love Thuy even when she is very sick." The activity also provided exposure to culture. Students compared and contrasted American marriage ceremonial traditions with those of their own countries.

I left the main office after signing out and started the short trek to my car. It was nearing five o'clock that autumn afternoon, the light already beginning to fade. I glanced to my right where the cheerleaders practiced in the cement courtyard. Hours earlier it had offered shade in the way of a long and narrow overhang. From the huddle of gangly females, Geovanny's small shape emerged, coming in my direction. I figured he'd missed the bus in order to hang with the eighth-grade cheerleader he'd had his eyes on recently. But then I noticed a slender woman trailing behind him. *His mother's onto his game,* I thought, wondering how much she knew of his flirtations.

As they drew close, it became clear exactly how stunning his mother was—almost Sophia Lorenesque. She wore hip-hugger jeans and a mustard-tweed jacket that complemented her olive complexion, brown shoulder-length hair, and large hazel eyes. The lack of family resemblance caught me off guard.

My briefcase, jam-packed with papers I intended to grade that evening, weighed me down. Tired, hungry, and anxious to get home, I fleetingly considered making a beeline for my car. Not fluent in Spanish, I generally tried to avoid any communication with parents after a long and exhausting day. But the professional part of me acquiesced. Geovanny's mother deserved to know, if she didn't already, about her son's weak literacy skills and hyperactivity. I set down my belongings to conduct a parent-teacher conference impromptu, right there outside the school's main entrance.

"Ms. Smith, my mama want speak with you," Geovanny announced as he approached. He grinned innocently, as if bracing himself and his mother for a glowing report. *He thinks he's too cute for me to say anything negative,* I thought.

"Oh," I feigned surprise. His mother and I greeted each other with a nod. Geovanny continued his proud beaming for either his mother or himself or both. Difficult to tell.

"Señora, gracias por venir." I smiled warmly as I thanked her for coming. She didn't return the smile, but she did appear eager to hear what I had to say.

I intentionally started, in my broken Spanish, with Geovanny's strengths—that her son was very funny and kept everyone laughing; that he was popular, especially with the girls, but with the boys too. Yet she didn't respond to my lighthearted compliments. Her intense look seemed to beg, *Tell me the real stuff.* By this point Geovanny's grin had

143

sagged a little. He fidgeted and looked from his mother to me.

Already flustered, I told Geovanny, "I'm going to speak in English, and I want you to tell your mom what I say in Spanish. Okay?" I trusted he had enough respect for her not to deliberately misinterpret the conversation.

I continued with the positive. "I like having Geovanny in my class. He is a good boy. Yes, he is playful, but he is respectful. He listens and follows the rules." This, Geovanny gladly interpreted. His mother gave a slight dip of her chin.

"He learns vocabulary quickly and has no fear of speaking English or of making mistakes in the process, which is how one learns." I said something to this effect, but mindful to simplify my language so Geovanny could carry out his role as interpreter. His mother seemed unimpressed with this part.

Then I moved on to my concerns. Geovanny had difficulty transitioning to independent work, shifting gears from comedian performance to classwork. Consequently, he rarely completed written assignments and his grades suffered. Yet I felt reluctant to fail him because his verbal skills indicated that he was acquiring English.

"Geovanny has a hard time reading and writing. Did he have problems learning to read in El Salvador?" I asked. Immigrant kids often entered U.S. schools with little documentation of their previous schooling. I hadn't been able to tell if Geovanny's challenges resulted from a disability or from a lack of a solid academic foundation. He exhibited qualities that fit the profile of a dyslexic student: clever, witty, creative, curious, perceptive, verbal, and active, but also inattentive to detail, unfocused, and quick to weary of activities that involved the written word. Then again, being from El Salvador, he might have had interrupted schooling.

Finally, the mother spoke. She mentioned no learning disability, blaming his literacy issues instead on his silliness and inability to pay attention. She assured me, locking her eyes with Geovanny's, that she would talk to his father about the excessive playfulness and make sure their son attended after-school tutoring one day a week. Geovanny didn't break his mother's gaze. Capitalizing on his unusual display of seriousness, I said that her son needed to think before he leapt, that his playfulness was getting him into trouble and could even get him hurt.

We parted ways. Faded streaks of light dripped down the November sky, watery inkblots in a painting. I drove home, satisfied with our exchange. Contacting Geovanny's parents had been on my mind for weeks. Now I could cross it off my list. I sensed that his mother had backbone. I smiled, recalling how Geovanny, grinning, had enjoyed the attention during the first part of the conference.

The next day, everything changed. The dry, sunny weather was devoured by dreary gray fog. Looking out the classroom windows, I couldn't distinguish sky from ground. First period began with a mere two students in attendance. *Where was everyone?* An intercom announcement interrupted the quiet: school bus 117, the one many of my students rode, had been delayed. Not terribly unusual, since this bus had the farthest distance to cover. It traveled the outlying, rural route of the school zone, dotted with trailer parks, random houses, yards scattered with chickens and rusted pickup trucks. Haphazard, narrow rutted roads, bordered by low-lying ditches, often got covered by a few inches of water, which made for slower going in bad weather. I altered my lesson so as not to get too far ahead.

Before long, I heard a few footsteps, the opening and closing of a few locker doors in the hallway. But the sounds were subdued. In fact, considering that a busload of kids had just set foot on the premises, the present quiet was almost eerie. I looked up, surprised to find three students—sisters

145

Paloma and Perla, and one of Geovanny's more serious girlfriends, María—peeking in from the doorway. The girls were in my seventh-period class, not my first one of the day. Soft-spoken and timid, the three would never think to enter a classroom unassigned to them. Yet clearly distraught, they marched one behind the other to my side.

"Ms. Smith, a car hit Geovanny on the bus stop," Perla blurted. Her hands shook as she gathered her long hair back from her face. María stood next to Perla, her eyes swollen from crying. Her lips and chin trembled.

"Did you see it?" I hoped this was one of those unfounded rumors that, from time to time, burst to the surface of middle-school life.

"Yes, we see it," Paloma answered. "Everyone. Everyone in the bus see it."

"Where is Geovanny now?" I asked.

"The *ambulancia* come and take to the hospital," María whispered.

My first-period students, now filing in, would require immediate attention. I told the girls, "Go to your class, but come back here for lunch. I'll go to the office and see what's happening. Don't worry. The hospital will take good care of Geovanny."

The two sisters, obedient by nature, left. But María lingered. Fragile on a normal day, she couldn't possibly manage the stress and noise of her first-period P.E. class. Needing to process, she started explaining in detail how the accident unfolded. Luckily, my students listened with rapt attention, aware of María and Geovanny's relationship.

A group of kids had been waiting at the bus stop on busy, six-lane Telephone Road. The bus not yet in sight, someone dared Geovanny to run to the 7-Eleven on the opposite side of the road, buy candy and chips, and run back before the bus took off. It wasn't in Geovanny's nature to ignore such a challenge. According to María, he made it across to the store, but then the bus arrived. My thoughts reeled to the previous evening when I'd warned his mother of his impulsive nature. I couldn't help but dwell on the uncanniness of the timing.

While Geovanny was sprinting back to catch the bus, a car skidded over the wet surface and struck him. The driver was an "old white lady" who immediately slumped over her steering wheel—most likely from the shock of hitting a child with her car. María demonstrated the woman's action by hunching her shoulders and putting her head on her folded arms. Geovanny's tennis shoes flew into the air from the impact. Geovanny himself also shot up then landed on the back of his head. The ambulance came quickly and took him away.

None of my first-period witnesses listening to María disagreed with her, so I assumed her version was accurate. When she finished, she begged me to call the hospital, but I told her it was too early. I let her stay in my classroom the entire day.

At my first free moment I dashed to the front office. The secretaries sat at their typewriters tight-lipped, eyes riveted to the keys they were pounding, oblivious to the commotion. The principal's door periodically opened as police officers came and went, their walkie-talkies blaring indecipherable phrases. No one seemed willing to talk or speculate. Feeling in the way, I left.

Around lunchtime the assistant principal came to my room and announced that Geovanny had been rushed into surgery as soon as he arrived at the hospital. He remained in surgery for the rest of the day, at least in our imaginations. That was our only news.

Over the next few months, sad but predictable updates on Geovanny's condition filtered into the classroom. He'd suffered a traumatic brain injury that left him unconscious for weeks, his possibility for recovery clouded in mystery.

After what I deemed an appropriate amount of time to wait—two weeks—I decided to visit him in the hospital on my way home. Stepping out of the elevator, I noticed a small crowd of people getting on another one. I gathered they were related to Geovanny, his handsome father holding the younger siblings in each hand, aunts, uncles, possibly grandparents. The gravity of Geovanny's situation abruptly hit me, how the lives of his family members had changed forever.

I expected to find him connected by tubes to machines and IV bags, in a windowless, cramped space with one or two chairs for visitors. Instead, oddly, he lay in a huge, open room. Floor-to-ceiling windows lined a front wall, offering abundant light to tall potted palms. His bed, the single piece of furniture in the room, had been positioned to the side of what resembled a center stage. Geovanny lay as if in a deep sleep, surrounded by burning candles on the floor and low tables. Flickering images of Jesus and of the Virgin Mary and other saints shone through the glass candles sealed with papier-mâché art.

And then I saw Geovanny's mother. In the shadowy light of the candles, her profile was still striking. Yet she didn't look the same. Obviously fatigued, but also as if bound to another universe. She nodded to me, maybe in faint recognition. She probably hadn't left her son's side since the accident. Her oldest, he'd been the light of her life, as he'd been the light of my classroom. She alternated between putting damp washcloths on Geovanny's forehead and keeping candles lit. He looked peaceful—the one saving grace. I didn't mean to stay long. Wishing I'd brought a candle and not a generic sympathy card, I squeezed his hand and tiptoed to the elevator.

The inescapable sadness of a shattered dream came over me. Many immigrants undertake a challenging journey for the purpose of following a dream, with the hope of improving their family's (or just their own) lot in life. The previous summer, during a visit to Ellis Island I'd spent time viewing a museum exhibit. On the walls hung stark black-and-white photos of immigrants from all walks of life arriving in New York by ship. They came with only a small suitcase, or a pack tied to their back. They stood in crowds or in lines, some appearing eager, but most of them obviously anxious and forlorn. I peered into each photo, hoping to find my sixteen-year-old Swedish great-grandmother. Geovanny's parents might have experienced similar hardship leaving El Salvador and bringing three young children to Houston, Texas, in search of a brighter future. Yet their oldest son's future now seemed anything but bright.

Geovanny awoke from his coma during Christmas break. After school resumed, I offered to take Paloma, Perla, and María to visit him. They didn't hesitate, but their urgency to see him had long passed. His accident had become old news. En route to the hospital, they hardly mentioned him or the accident. In fact, they giggled and teased each other as if headed to the mall or a movie.

We found Geovanny in the same room and bed where I'd seen him before. But the devotional prayer candles, and his mother, weren't there. He greeted us with large, watchful eyes. If the girls had any concerns, they masked them well.

"Geovanny, what's up?" Paloma asked.

"How you like here?" asked Perla.

"Everybody in the class say hi and they miss you," María said. "They wanna know when you coming back."

Geovanny's vacant stare traveled from girl to girl as each took a turn speaking. They showed him the get-well cards students had made. Filling the awkward silence, they slowly read the messages written inside, pointing to the words. Unsure if Geovanny understood what they were saying, the girls pressed on to other topics, mainly jokes or current news about friends. The right side of his mouth now drooped downward, but I thought I detected a glimmer of a smile.

In a very short time, the girls ran out of things to say, and we stood to leave. They promised to return soon and to bring others with them. As we said our goodbyes, he raised his hand inches from his bedsheet, an attempt to wave.

Geovanny came back to school in a wheelchair on a Monday at the tail end of the spring semester. Many students had seen him around the neighborhood, so his altered condition didn't shock them. But he was a totally different Geovanny. He rode the special needs bus. He wore a diaper, though few people knew that. He drooled and struggled to communicate out of one side of his mouth. His hand movements were tense and spastic. What remained unchanged were his soulful eyes.

That Monday, several of us, excited about his return, visited with him in the courtyard during lunch. Those soulful eyes of his now held a soft merriment.

But our midday reunion took place only on his first day back. As always, the end of school was a busy time, and the kids got tied up with closing out library fines, returning textbooks, and attending award ceremonies and talent shows.

Geovanny's academic plan the following year, seventh grade for him, included placement in the self-contained classroom with the other physically disabled students. His full-time aide wheeled him to my room each day for forty-five minutes of mandated ESL instruction. My strongest memory of this arrangement is of a day when Geovanny and his aide arrived amidst a particularly energetic hubbub of activity. Students in groups of four rewrote texts on large sheets of paper, substituting random words with hand-drawn pictures. For example, instead of writing *eyes*, they might replace it with .

Students shouted suggestions, rapidly exchanging

ideas, completely engaged in their poster production. Only one group acknowledged Geovanny, and that was simply to slide their chairs over to make room for his bulky wheelchair, which fit only at the end of a table. He sat apart and watched, his aide seated beside him—both of them observers, not participants.

I stepped up to the table and said, "Ask Geovanny to pick a word for you to draw." María responded by showing Geovanny on his copy the relevant line in the text. But he couldn't read or hold the text, and to *speak* even a single word took painfully long. The students, caught up in the moment, didn't have the wherewithal to slow down. Nor did I.

Gratefully, I found a way for Geovanny to participate when the class gathered to present their pictographs. I handed him my metal pointer, and he traced lines while someone read aloud. Yet it was apparent that Geovanny wasn't in sync with the reader, but was simply going through the motions. Still, the fact that he was contributing outweighed the downside of students getting confused.

At the onset of his return after the accident, Geovanny focused on and followed people's movements and conversations. His eyes indicated that he was connecting, although, since speech was impossible, he reacted with groans. Yet, little by little, he gave up. I couldn't help but wonder if he realized how his role had diminished. Did he remember how easily he once commanded an audience, or how he made his classmates laugh at the drop of a hat? His attendance in my ESL class became more sporadic and then stopped altogether. It did seem pointless. After that, the only regular interaction I observed between Geovanny and my students became a wave of the hand from afar in a hall, the cafeteria, a courtyard. He slipped away from us like a helium balloon floating higher and higher until it becomes a speck in the sky.

I did visit Geovanny in his self-contained classroom

from time to time during his eighth-grade year, and I hoped his peers did as well. He grew taller of course, and small hairs sprouted on his chin and upper lip. Whenever I entered the room, his eyes lit up, giving proof to the connection and memories that remained. And for that I felt a twinge of gratitude.

Harmony: Few Words Required

How was your Christmas? What did Santa bring you? How was your spring break? What did you do? Did you go out of town? Did you have fun? Teachers and administrators, although well intentioned, never failed to bombard students with a litany of questions when they returned from a school break. Once, after a first day back overhearing too many exchanges between adults and kids in halls and classrooms that began with those kinds of questions, I became inspired to write a chant to teach to my students. It was really a simple back-and-forth conversation asking general "how" questions: *How's your mother? How's school? How are your classes? etc.*

Students practiced reading then reciting the chant in groups and in pairs. But something organically happened that I hadn't anticipated. The chant took on a life of its own as the kids, being adolescents naturally predisposed to rebelliousness and defiance, started substituting my original positive responses with more negative ones. Here's the final product—a rewrite on their part, and one they gladly took ownership of.

How are you?
I'm bad.

How's your mother?
She's terrible.

How's your brother?
He's sad.

How's school?
It's boring.

How are your classes?
They're stupid.

How was your vacation?
It sucked!!

The final line they shouted in perfect unison. *Sucked* approaches forbidden language, and so they were exercising their freedom to say a bad word in a formal setting. But more significantly, their emphasis on that last line of the chant made an impression on me. I developed a sneaking suspicion that some of them truly did have sucky vacations. I came to realize that their responses of "boring" or "nothing" to questions about how they'd spent their vacation were genuine. That they weren't acting as typical adolescents do, too apathetic to elaborate for the inquiring adult on the fun they'd had. My students actually did sit in front of a TV for a large part of their school breaks.

I'm not implying that more interactive activities never happened in their homes. Yet they probably did less frequently than in the homes of nonimmigrants. The majority of my students' parents or guardians had jobs in service industries. They slept during the day and worked nights. Since most of them didn't have holidays off, they couldn't supervise or entertain their children during vacations. Immigrant families, in fear of *La Migra*—being picked up at a bus stop or grocery store and deported—felt compelled to keep their children close by. Travel or day trips were made difficult by the fact that parents, mothers especially, didn't necessarily own a car or have a driver's license. Nor did families have easy access to the internet or to computers that worked. Their children experienced isolation, boredom, and possibly hunger, since school being out meant no free cafeteria lunches.

Of course, I wished a different trajectory for my students. Any inroads I could make seemed minor, but still worth something. At least, that's what my gut told me, in the form of an epiphany. So, on the eve of the next school vacation, which happened to be the winter break that started right before Christmas, I collected home phone numbers from my newest—and, thus, least connected—students. For some reason, they all happened to be Burmese. I guessed that a cluster of Burmese families had recently been cleared for entry by the State Department and then some local church had managed to get them settled in Austin.

"Do you want to go to a Christmas light show on Sunday?" I asked them. "It is far. We have to go in my car." Heads nodded, a few smiles appeared—although I had no way of knowing what they'd understood.

It occurred to me that a student helper might come in handy. Someone who could help to bridge communication and model what to do. Amy came to mind. From Beijing, Amy (her "American" name, Lifen being her actual one) knew English to a certain degree and had chalked up some life experiences. I hoped she'd agree to be that bridge for us, and luckily she did.

"Write down your phone number. I will call your parents on Saturday," I instructed the four students, passing out slips of paper. By the end of the class I had them in my possession. I was now committed to this project of mine.

On Saturday I sat down to make the calls, leading off with Amy since I'd communicated with her mother before. Amy herself picked up on the first ring. She handed the receiver to her mother, who assured me Lifen would be ready and waiting the next afternoon in the Building D parking lot of their apartment complex. Her detailed instructions in English on where to pick up her daughter seemed rehearsed.

Although encouraged by this first response, I still didn't put much stock in the field trip actually transpiring. The Burmese families would be harder, considering the huge language gap and the fact that information often got lost in translation from school to home—especially when it was over the course of two days. I braced myself for no answers or wrong numbers or non-English-speaking people answering the phone then hanging up.

I dialed the number of Naing Ye, who had enrolled in my class a mere two weeks earlier. Again, the person on the other end answered almost instantly. I introduced myself. "Hello? I am Naing Ye's English teacher—" That was as far as I got. Static, muffled sounds, then faint, indistinct voices. I imagined someone, fumbling in confusion, pressing the receiver into a couch cushion. "Hello?" I repeated. I knew to practice patience.

"Teacher, my friend want talk you," came a timid young female voice, possibly Aung Reh's. Lo and behold, the friend, an adult who spoke exceptional English with a thick accent, turned out to be one of two Burmese interpreters who worked within the community. He gave his permission for the trip and conveniently offered to make arrangements with the remaining families. I've often wondered if the interpreter's presence had been coincidental or if he'd visited Naing Ye's home that afternoon solely to coordinate the event. Whatever was happening in the privacy of their homes, my four students had been smoothly cleared for passage. I was thrilled.

Picking up the students at three different apartment

complexes on Sunday afternoon proved seamless as well. We set out in my tiny, and now overloaded, Ford Aspire to a small town twenty miles away. As we drove along the two-lane highway, the sky darkened. The gloomy afternoon felt chilly and damp. An awkward silence wasted no time seeping into the crowded space. There was no dominant language. I spoke English, of course, and intermediate Spanish. The three newest students spoke a Burmese language, although not necessarily the same one, and zero English. And Amy spoke Mandarin and basic English, which at least allowed her and me a few brief exchanges of pleasantries. An only child and precocious, Amy commanded a comfort level with adults that bordered on presumptuousness. And yet today I felt grateful for her presence.

The kids stared out the windows and coughed quietly into their jacket sleeves. I found myself questioning my decision to carry out this undertaking. *What was I thinking? How can my students have fun when they can't talk to one another or to me?* Brushing aside my familiar self-doubt, I told myself that these young Christian passengers would embrace the festive light show with its multiple displays of Baby Jesus in the manger surrounded by Mary, Joseph, the Wise Men, and shepherds.

As I drove—no background chatter to distract me—I revisited my belief that childhood memories provide lifelong satisfaction and that shared experiences help create them. This belief was reflected in what I did in the classroom. I favored human interaction, resisting a fundamental push for the use of technology. A language teacher dedicated to communication, I hadn't gotten sucked into technology's enticements: the stimulating animation and colorful graphics, the bells and whistles and instant feedback. Computers require less emotional input. A daily segment of my ninety-minute lessons involved students talking face to face in a circle without the distractions of electronics or even pencil and paper. They participated in oral drills, question and answer sessions, open-ended discussions, and games. Students listened to, repeated, inquired of, agreed or disagreed with each other. And—learning aside—speaking activities, because of the spontaneity inherent in them, produced moments of laughter, tenderness, and bonding.

The four travelers and I arrived at our destination at dusk, the first car in the gravel parking lot. Meandering along the cedar-chip pathway lined with strings of white lights, we passed small replicas of buildings from bygone years. They were adorned with painted wooden reindeer, Mr. and Mrs. Clauses, lollipops, elves and sleighs, wreaths and stockings. We approached an area containing artistically crafted xylophones and steel drums. My students played the instruments until they got annoyed by a family with six children who tried to join in. We moved on.

The trail twisted in crazy-eight fashion, leading up wobbly stone steps to its very top. By now it was dark. There was a light breeze that we paused to take in, along with the expansive vista of two looming mesas in shadow and the brilliant crescent moon that hung between them. Long strands of lights, angled between the top of a high pole and the ground, gently swayed; we stood in the center of this semblance of a Christmas tree, enclosed by twinkling brightness. Looking up to the open sky, we spun around. Tha Zaw got dizzy enough to fall and the giggling began. We now shared a universal feeling, awestruck by light and wind, hills and moon.

At that moment Naing Ye whipped out a disposable camera he must have purchased for the outing. The kids instantly contorted their bodies, twisting into crazy poses—group poses, poses in a sleigh, poses with a snowman, poses with me, poses without me. The laughing snowballed.

With the film used up, we strolled back down the steps toward another focal point, a massive bonfire. People of all ages sat on logs sipping hot chocolate from Styrofoam cups. Others roasted hot dogs with metal prongs. A youth choir sang "Joy to the World" on a makeshift stage to the left of the bonfire. Parents and grandparents wrapped in blankets watched from bleachers. Before I'd even suggested it, the kids grabbed a utensil and a hot dog from a table and found their way to an available space at a slow-burning log. They observed a little girl rotate her hot dog inches above a low flame and followed suit. Just as Tha Zaw lifted his to eat it, it fell to the ground. More laughter. The others timidly nibbled at their own, but most of the meat ended up in the trash. The group returned from the refreshment area with cups of hot chocolate, bringing one for me. We sipped our steamy drinks and people-watched, taking in this very traditional American holiday scene.

The camera session, food, and fire had warmed my students to each other. Without having to speak, we tossed our cups into a barrel and eased our way to the remaining portion of the trail. It was then that Naing Ye's curiosity overcame him. He tried to grab a present wrapped in red paper and green ribbon perched precariously on top of Santa's sleigh—only to discover it wasn't a present at all, but rather a metal canister painted red and green for effect. His misdeed drew the biggest laughter of the evening by far. Amy shrieked in disbelief, convulsing in laughter, hair covering her face. Older and more cosmopolitan, Amy had spent her pre-America life in Beijing excelling at mathematics and taking private voice lessons. Naing Ye had, until a month ago, lived in a refugee camp in Thailand near its border with Burma (or Myanmar, as the country is also called). Worlds apart, but now they found themselves together in a Texas town celebrating Christmas.

At this point the kids seemed intent on seeking out one last diversion—something to delay reaching the end of this special time. And then that perfect something emerged from behind low trees: a monstrous dark statue, impossibly large to go unnoticed. The Burmese students hesitated in its shadow but then slowly moved toward it, spellbound. Only

Amy hung back, not fearful as much as disinterested, the result of too many visits to theme parks. The film in Naing Ye's disposable camera suddenly wasn't used up, and they took a few final pictures again in different combinations: next to, between the legs of, and in front of the life-size dinosaur.

As we piled into the car, I had a hard time believing I was in the company of the same kids I'd picked up a short time ago. We hadn't even left the parking lot before the singing commenced. Maybe the performance at the bonfire had inspired them. Amy initiated the first round of songs with one in Chinese. Several verses flowed rapidly from deep in her throat. Not understanding the lyrics or knowing whether the ballad was Christmas-related or not, the rest of us were captivated by the stream of words. We listened effortlessly. Next, Naing Ye burst into song. I was delighted. *What twelve-year-old American boy would do this?* Aung Reh followed with her own sweet melody. My four students introduced song after song, politely allowing each other their moment to shine.

For one of her turns, Amy chose an American spiritual I'd introduced to the class early in the school year. "I've got peace like a river, I've got peace like a river, I've got peace like a river in my soul," she began. Three more stanzas, all error-free, followed. This became my moment to shine, and I blushed with teacher pride. (Fortunately, in the darkness no one noticed.) Since in the classroom Amy often met my unorthodox teaching methodologies with comments like "this so silly" or "this idea crazy" followed by a slight snicker, her eagerness to sing the river song surprised me. And her perfect recall, her perfect tune and cadence, gave me validation, in its purest form, of a notion I clung to—that adolescents initially resist what they sometimes wind up appreciating the most.

As happens on long rides, the kids became increasingly uninhibited about their musical selections and

160

singing abilities. Suddenly, in four-part harmony they belted out a few lines from that overdone Justin Bieber song: "baby, baby, baby, oh . . . baby, baby, baby, no." With their individual pronunciations of baby, it sounded nothing short of hilarious, a symphony of diverse accents coming together for a short rendition of American pop music. I credited Naing Ye for launching "Baby." He led the group into this grand finale with the only English song they could have sung together. Sadly, there's no recording of their impromptu sing-along. It took place before cell phones became an appendage of bodies. The moment was lost somewhere in time and space and is now only a distant memory.

None of the four students ever spoke of our adventure to see Christmas lights. At least to me they didn't. The next year Amy's stepfather died from a lingering cancer. She and her mother moved in with a friend living in a nearby town, and we didn't keep in touch. Aung Reh transferred schools her seventh-grade year.

Naing Ye also spent seventh grade at another middle school, but returned to my school for eighth grade.

"Remember me, Miss?" he asked, his eyes searching mine, on his first day back.

"Of course I do," I answered, although, truth be told, it took me a minute. He'd matured from a goofy youngster trying to open fake Christmas presents and singing Justin Bieber songs in his teacher's car, into a lanky teenager with orange spiked hair, dressed in goth-style clothes, chains and leather, with a skateboard in tow. Now he had poise, combined with an understated but very real drive to learn English and be a top-notch student.

My intuition tells me that as immigrant kids assimilate into American culture, they experience a strong pull to disassociate from their former selves. They avoid reminders of what they were like when they first came to the

161

United States. They want to fit in, and any suggestion to the contrary brings them an element of shame. And yet, even though none of those four students ever acknowledged that Christmas holiday field trip, I feel certain they remembered it. After all, Amy clearly hadn't forgotten the four stanzas to a song written in a foreign language and learned three months earlier. She simply needed the right combination of privacy and intimacy to acknowledge it.

Food for Thought

"What is the difference between *a* and *the*? They both are singular." The person confused about those special adjectives called articles wasn't a student, but a colleague and friend of mine. Her name was Aya Goodwin (born and raised in Japan, but married to an American), and we'd shared classrooms and portables for years. She taught Japanese language classes and Japanese fine arts, and now she was enrolled in an online program to add ESL to her repertoire of teaching certifications. A requirement of the program was to write thirty essays in thirty days. I had agreed, as her former mentor teacher, to serve as editor-in-chief. Helping Aya with her writing proved a welcome change from teaching English at its most basic level.

      While going over her daily essays, I'd repeatedly substituted the indefinite article *a* for the definite article *the* and vice versa, or added one of them when it was lacking. Her usual response to any of my grammar revisions went something like this: "Yeah, yeah, yeah. Okay. Thank you sooo much. I will make corrections right away." Then she'd hurry off to the night class she taught at a community college or to one of her four children's after-school programs. Yet every so often—as in the case of *a* versus *the*—she'd slow

163

down long enough to ask, "But why? Why do you say it like that?" This gave me permission to play linguist, a favorite pastime, and she and I would break into a lively discussion. Aya, an ESL learner herself, also appreciated the nuances of language.

I got why Aya struggled with articles. They don't exist in Japanese. Nor was Aya the only one who confused them. I began to notice that my more advanced ESL students could also benefit from a grammar lesson on the topic. (In fact, one of the sixteen Language Arts Benchmark items had recently tested identification of the correct article.) It was a no-brainer. I would use the same lesson format with my students that I'd created for Aya.

Here was her simple lesson: "Can you hand me *a* book?" I requested and swept my hand over several books I'd placed on a table. Aya nodded and immediately grabbed the one closest to her. This indicated her understanding that it didn't matter which book she chose. Then I removed all of them except one. "Can you hand me *the* book, please?" I said, pointing to the only book remaining. "You see? *A* means any one object or person from a group, while *the* refers to that one, and only that specific one," I explained.

After more demonstrations using pencils and pens and paper clips, Aya had responded, with her accent that I'd come to love, "Oh, now I understand. Yes. I see."

Honestly, I was flabbergasted when Aya received nothing below an A- on the thirty essays. From my point of view, the number of first-language interference errors they contained impeded comprehension. I wondered whether I'd been over-critiquing Aya's speech and writing. Had I become a stickler for accuracy, both with Aya and my students? If higher education institutions had relaxed their standards of English usage, this would translate to immigrant students' easier access to college and university opportunities. I should welcome such a trend.

Several weeks after our mini-lesson on definite and

indefinite articles, something happened that underlined the importance of using precise language. Aya had asked a Japanese painter who was touring Texas to speak to her fine arts class, and she'd invited her students' parents to the talk. On the morning of, I overheard her scrambling next door, opening closets and drawers and banging them shut. At the last minute she'd decided to host the artist in the school library rather than her classroom. Through the window I watched her post a note on her door before she rushed off. My guess was that it directed students and parents to the library.

Soon I noticed clumps of people moseying down the portable's wooden ramp. They gathered at Aya's door, read the sign, then lingered, glancing around, unsure of what to do or where to go. I opened my door and, from there, read the taped note flapping in the breeze.

I am at a library. Please meet there.

The school had a single library, yet Aya had implied that more than one existed. So, *which* library became the question. "Ms. Goodwin's class is in the library today," I assured the crowd, waving in its general direction. The students, sure of the location of the one and only library, breathed a sigh of relief and motioned for their parents to follow them.

Admittedly, I felt responsible for Aya's mistake. If I hadn't bothered to highlight her misuse and nonuse of articles, she might have written "I am at library. Please go there." Incorrect, but less confusing.

Aya's note reaffirmed my belief that language instruction deserved top priority. It was a belief that didn't sit well with my higher-ups, who mandated content-driven instruction even for ESL learners. An underlying assumption existed that such students would innately acquire English while they read myths and biographies, wrote compositions, or attempted any other learning objective required of them in their language arts class—which was their ESL class. In my students' reality, subject-based knowledge superseded sequential, effectual language learning. As a result, they acquired English haphazardly.

My experience taught me that this piecemeal and frankly inefficient approach to language instruction works only with a small segment of the population. Most learners after the age of twelve require explicit instruction and lots of practice time to learn a language—conditions not afforded my students. Practice involves time, and time equals money. Public education remains underfunded and steered by an accountability movement that demands fast, tangible results in the form of improved test scores. When I didn't listen to my own voice of reason, I would, for instance, spend hours teaching students to identify a correct multiple-choice answer of a summary (one that has a beginning, middle, and end) rather than provide them guided practice with recently introduced grammatical forms. I sacrificed building students' confidence and their abilities to comprehend, speak, read, and write English well—needed lifelong skills—for the prospect of answering test items correctly on an end-of-year test.

Observing and interacting with Aya Goodwin over the years prompted me at times to reflect on other aspects of my instructional practices besides teaching grammar—aspects from the mundane to the philosophical.

An example of the mundane? The way Aya took attendance, which was so very different from my own routine. For her, it was the first order of business, carried out in the exact same fashion every day. Since I occasionally listened in, I knew what it sounded like.

"Rodney-*san*," she read from the class roll. No inflection, impassive as a robot.

"*Hai*," answered Rodney, somewhat animated. (In their very first class of Japanese, students had, of course, been taught how to say "yes.")

"Shaneka-*san*."

"*Hai*," Shaneka responded.

"Carly-*san*."

No response. Aya paused, staring at her paper list, patiently waiting. She deliberated five seconds, made a red line on the paper, and moved on.

"Dustin-*san*."

"*Hai*," Dustin replied.

Here's how I, a laissez-faire American and by nature not big on detail, took roll. When I had a free moment, I would eyeball my class silently and mark the absentees directly in the computer attendance system. "Where's [missing student]?" I'd ask offhandedly. Often I forgot to take attendance at all—not a good habit for a public school teacher, as funding is dependent on numbers of students present.

Most ESL classrooms are microcosms in terms of accents, and my own classrooms were no exception. Aya helped me to formulate an appreciation for accents. Hers was thick. On plenty of occasions I had no idea what she was saying, including when we once carpooled to an overnight faculty retreat. The hour-long drive gave us time to catch up after a busy summer break. I discovered that she'd traveled to Tokyo, as she did most summers to visit her aging father, and had brought along two of her four children.

"And when I was there, *everyone* keeps asking me about famous American," Aya recounted. "Actor, maybe. Or something like that. He's very, very famous. Everyone in Japan is in love with him, but I'm not sure I can say the name. It's, um, Hally Botty. Or something like that." After she made several more attempts to pronounce it, I suggested,

"Halle Berry?"—though not really convinced that Berry, although beautiful and famous, was a high-caliber celebrity in Japan.

"He's man?" Aya asked.

"No, Halle Berry is a woman. An actress."

"No, I'm talking about boy. He's young, like teenager. He wears big glasses."

"Oh! Harry Potter!"

"Yes! Exactly!" she exclaimed, and we had the giggles for a good while as we suffered through Austin traffic.

Accents can be a source of frustration for people, but they're also entertaining. For me, they added richness and spice to the language classroom. Eventually I focused less on pronunciation, my philosophy being that the world would be pretty boring if everyone spoke with the same accent or sentence patterns.

I also admired Aya's dedication to biculturalism, an inherent part of the ESL classroom. (I hoped that my admiration manifested itself as an awareness to encourage my students to do the same.) Aya seemed to equally cherish Japanese and American cultures. Each summer in Tokyo she alternated registering two of her four American-born children in a summer school program to study Japanese, determined that they maintain some of their heritage. The exquisite dresses from Tokyo that Aya wore looked otherworldly; yet on Fridays she donned a plaid country-western shirt, hip-hugger jeans, and leather boots, looking as Texan as the rest of us. She pounced on any new Japanese restaurant, dragging her children across town to check it out; but she was also the first to suggest a McDonald's Big Mac for lunch.

"How did you end up living in the U.S.?" I asked her one day, assuming that a job or a college exchange program had brought her here.

"I knew when I was little girl, I would live in

America someday. I just knew it. I loved music and fashions of America. Growing up, I had posters of national parks on every wall of my bedroom. Of New York City and San Francisco too. And I really wanted to marry American." She confided this last part with a chuckle.

"So, I met my husband when I was traveling in California. Then we moved to Austin together, because he is from here. That was fifteen years ago. And here still I am."

On occasion, I observed Aya introduce assignments. They had the "feel" of a contract more than a school project. She'd hand each student a copy, drawn up on a single sheet of paper, the criteria and deadlines clearly spelled out, then proceed to read it aloud in a monotone voice, not once diverting from the text.

What was missing for me, as an American teacher, was the sales pitch. For Aya, there was no sense of responsibility to engage students, to get them excited about their assignment, to earn "buy-in." Inspiring students seemed as far off her radar as it was foremost on mine. At the conclusion of a project, something parallel took place— or, rather, didn't take place. In most American classrooms, teachers frequently praise students with "great job," "awesome," "you rock," etc. etc. (whether deserved or not). Not Aya. Students might receive a barely audible "good job" from her after they'd delivered a presentation that took them hours to prepare.

In her initial years in public education, Aya had many a conference with the principal over her high failure rate. Administrators called into question teachers with a set percentage of students who didn't pass their course, implying that the instructor was partly at fault. An administrator might review a teacher's clarity of expectations, her management style, whether she presented information in a meaningful or relevant way. I wondered how much self-examination went on in Aya's head. She would return from these meetings irritated over any suggestion that she assume blame for her students failing to turn in assignments by her clearly communicated deadlines.

To Aya's credit, over time she adapted. She integrated hands-on activities into her lessons, considered a must for anyone teaching an elective as well as a valued methodology in American education circles. Students in her Japanese fine arts classes created and presented haikus with props, made Japanese kites and flew them on the football fields, wrote Japanese characters with ink on special paper, prepared traditional foods, and watched anime films.

A hard worker and a rule-abiding person, eventually Aya began to painstakingly document accommodations she made for specific students. She became a pro at knowing her students with learning disabilities and their required modifications. Her deadlines became less rigid. She stopped penalizing students who, for whatever reason, didn't come up with four dollars to pay for the ink to inscribe Japanese characters.

Aya's seeming reluctance (or was it confusion?) to start making allowances for students gave me pause. Had it been a function of her personality? Maybe to some degree, but I think it was more a function of environment—that she had come from a homogeneous society whose standards aren't adjusted but rather aspired to. Her origins were in a culture in which teachers enjoy authority, and their judgment and expertise are adhered to and trusted.

I sometimes found myself wishing I could operate like the "original" Aya, wishing to be Japanese at least for a day. How nice not to agonize over my students' level of engagement. I, unlike Aya, inherently took ownership when a fair number of students performed poorly on a test or project I'd administered. And I felt uneasy about my tendency to accommodate my students, their whims and hardships.

I posed to myself the same question I'd pondered about Aya: Was it a function of my personality that I found adhering to consistency, with regard to my students, to be such a challenge? Ambiguity is familiar to me as an individual, but also as an American. My culture claims to value tolerance, diversity, equal opportunity—goals that are sometimes at odds with the sense of uniformity present in other societies. Our public school administrators, not just our teachers, grapple with establishing effective disciplinary protocols and enforcing them in the same way with every student. (Plenty of students are granted second, third, sometimes even fourth chances; and by then everyone has entered the realm of "mixed messages.")

Ultimately Aya and I grew into our individual teaching styles. They took time to solidify and were always works in progress. But I feel lucky that we had each other. We were "food for thought" for each other. We stretched one another. I hope that teachers nowadays continue to have such working relationships, that the nature of the business still allows for this. Because an introspective teacher is an evolving teacher.

Months after I retired, I had a sudden urge to catch up with Aya and called her. She told me she'd been sick recently and had gone "to hospital" and "to doctor." I smiled, remembering our mini-lesson on articles. Yet even more so, my smile was in response to everything I'd gained from working alongside her all those years.

Ángel or *Diablo*?

My first students of the day sat in a circle waiting for Luis to bustle through the door. An eighth-grader with mannerisms of an old man, Luis seemed to accept his always-ten-minutes-behind as how his life was to run its course. I too had made my peace with his constant tardiness.

Half awake, he dragged a chair to the circle and slumped into it. He positioned himself slightly off-center as a protective measure from his partner in crime, Yanira. Both from Cuba, they had developed a playful friendship. Yanira soon stirred from her stupor, rolling her eyes in disapproval of Luis. When this didn't get his attention, she knocked her foot against his. Slowly, a dimply grin formed on Luis's sleepy face and his huge eyes took shape.

On some mornings, if I myself was resisting embarking on the busyness of the day, I let Yanira's and Luis's guttural Spanish rise to a turbulent frenzy. The other students and I would watch them, entranced by their gestures and animated language, the speed of which made it hard even for the Mexican Spanish speakers to follow. Their lively back and forth was entertaining yet disconcerting since, forced to speculate at what was being said, we never knew whether to expect hugs between them or chairs being thrown.

The students I taught from Cuba intrigued me—even

Miguel Ángel Morales Fuentes, my worst nightmare (every teacher has one) and the protagonist of this chapter. Miguel Ángel had immigrated to the United States as a refugee in the middle of fifth grade with his parents and younger brother. I met him at the onset of his sixth-grade year. Slight in stature, his skin the color of coffee with cream, he still exuded the preciousness of a young child. His parents kept his hair shaved, exposing a perfectly round head. Huge brown eyes and curly eyelashes covered half his face. His smile, a stark contrast to his usual scowl, warmed my heart. Over the course of the three years I taught him, I came to learn that that smile meant mischief. But it didn't stop me from melting whenever it surfaced.

Miguel Ángel's cleverness gained him leverage among his peers and me. Adept at acquiring oral language, he could get any point across in broken English. He was gifted as well with a keen perception and a curious mind.

One morning my students had suffered through an unimaginative paragraph about the ocean, which they seemed glad to put to rest. But not Miguel Ángel. Right when we were ready to move on, he became engrossed, having made a connection with information he'd heard elsewhere. He launched into a detailed explanation of how scientists were learning to extract salt from saltwater. "Yeah. Hey, Miss. You know the *científicos*, they gonna learn to take the *sal* from the water so the earth gonna have more water. They gonna build big *máquinas* to do this and . . ."

I welcomed Miguel Ángel's participation, even if it prolonged the lesson. Few of my students had the English skills to elaborate in this way. His passion infused others, and his English contained enough cognates that the Spanish speakers more or less understood him.

The challenge with Miguel Ángel lay in persuading him to read and write. He rarely put pen to paper, and when he did, he spelled his name *Migue Ange*. Dropping the final consonant in words possibly indicates dyslexia or dysgraphia or both, which could also have explained his strength in oral language. He never had a pencil—at least, one that was usable. He destroyed the points on purpose. Circling the room as students worked independently, I invariably found Miguel Ángel with his head down on the table, feigning sleep or playing a video game on a tablet hidden in his lap.

Whenever I prodded him, he'd gripe. "Miss, I already tol' you I don't have no pencil and I already know the answer. So why I have to write? That so stupid."

"Well, what *is* the answer?" I'd ask, genuinely curious.

In one such instance, the question involved identifying a character's motive. "The girl . . ." he started.

"You mean, the main character?" I interjected, trying to boost his use of academic vocabulary.

"Yeah, whatever. The girl she feel too bad she know too much English now and she don't want the cousins come to the play at the school. 'Cause she feel embarrass of his English."

Impressed with his intuition, I grabbed my own pen, and wrote verbatim what Miguel Ángel had said. He read it back to me. If he wasn't going to write, at least he could practice reading. It was a teachable moment. Yet fifteen other students around the room required attention.

"Now I want you to copy, onto *your* paper, your response I just wrote," I told him, then moved to the next table of students. Not for a minute did I believe he'd carry out the task without my direct supervision, but it seemed worth a try. Anything to get him into the habit of writing.

Miguel Ángel naturally became the classroom techie, the student most skilled in technology. It helped that he had tools at his disposal—flash drives, an iPod, a Gameboy, the most current cell phone. Many a morning, the sun barely up, the second I turned the key to enter my portable, boys rushed in silence to the computers lined against the wall. Once the machines were humming along, only then would the group notice the techie's absence.

One time Benito, head resting on elbow, let out a long sigh. "Miss, where's Miguel Ángel?"

"It's only 7:20. Why are you waiting for him?" I asked, interrupting my preparation of the day's lessons.

"He have the password," Rigoberto explained in mild exasperation. The kids had set their alarms a half hour early to come play a video game with Miguel Ángel before school, and now they had to wait.

Soon enough he arrived and set his overstuffed backpack on a desk. It teetered on the edge as he practically tore open the pocket that held the much-awaited flash drive. A sense of urgency prevailed as first period drew near—only twenty minutes to go.

Miguel Ángel admonished the group, something he could get away with as the key player. "I tol' you yesterday. You don't need no password. You can download the app. For free. Then you enter a password for you. I tol' you, but you don't listen. Man, you waste too much time. Now you got, like, fifteen minute to play. Dang, why you wait for me?" On and on he went, shaking his head, shaming the group.

A long time back I'd proclaimed myself off duty from refereeing conflicts before school. Students knew to keep the noise level and their demands of me to a minimum or else they'd lose their computer privileges. I couldn't resist eavesdropping though, always happy to hear their English progressing. Miguel Ángel's was especially remarkable— the blending of street language mixed with technical terms and idioms like "wasting time."

His computer expertise gained him a school-wide reputation as a kid who required heavy supervision. He downloaded illegal apps wherever he went, creating viruses and causing computers to shut down, always managing to stay one step ahead of the school technician. Whenever he was in the library, Ms. Roche maintained a hawk-eyed view of his computer screen from her position at the main counter. But the battle proved hopeless. As if he had eyes in the back of his head, he'd shift to the appropriate program nanoseconds before she approached his side, only to resume his video game or YouTube selection once she turned her back. This version of cat-and-mouse never let up, neither one willing to give it a rest.

Since I was forty years his senior, Miguel Ángel intuited my lack of confidence with technology, and he quickly learned to take advantage of it. One day he saw me panic when I'd inadvertently deleted a file. "Dude, don't worry," he told me with a grin, clicking through a series of icons. "You can never lose data." Admittedly, I relied on his savviness. When nobody else was able to download an article or resurrect the sound from a movie, he corrected the problem—that is, if he was willing.

Relinquishing control to Miguel Ángel over technology didn't always serve me well—like the time he tricked me into showing an offensive video to the class. At the start of the lesson that day, he sensed my good mood. Thrilled that the beginner ESL students sat ready to delve into their first chapter book, I handed out paper copies of *The Giving Tree* by Shel Silverstein. Each page contained a rudimentary sketch, depicting the text. The drawings, along with the simple vocabulary and repetitive language, helped readers' comprehension. I was eager to build my students' confidence and to engage them with the universal themes of the book, which I considered to be friendship and aging.

I opened *The Giving Tree* lesson, waving a hardcover copy for everyone to see. From his perch on the favored beanbag, Miguel Ángel instantly transformed from the reluctant reader who turned his back at the sight of a book to an animated, breathless child. Raising both hands, he shouted, "Oh, I know this story. The little boy visit the tree every day. They're friends. The tree give an apple to him. Then the boy cut down the tree at the end and miss the tree."

He'd summarized the story perfectly, adding, when

I probed about the theme, "The book talk 'bout making friends, you know, like, *amistades*. And 'bout getting old." Fortunately, due to the rest of his classmates' lack of English, he hadn't spoiled the story for them by revealing the ending. Instead, his excitement raised the curiosity level—a welcome bonus in a class of resistant readers.

I can't believe Miguel Ángel's reading books on his own, I thought, *particularly classics like* The Giving Tree.

"Miss Smit, let's watch the video," Miguel Ángel pleaded. "Is good. Like, five times I see it. My little brother, he love it too." Though disappointed, I took some satisfaction in his video viewing and hoped he might be inspired to read the book.

"Please, Miss, please. All the students gonna love it."

"Well, we have to *read* the story first," I told him, referring to a well-established rule: *read, then watch.* "If we finish the story in time, then we can see the video." He not only acquiesced but repositioned himself in the beanbag so he could easily follow the text—something I'd never seen him do.

With Miguel Ángel on board, the others joined in. I began reading the story aloud, and soon I had my audience in rapt attention. Then he raised his hand, volunteering to read, without prompting—another new behavior. To avoid interruption, I silently nodded to him. Without missing a beat, he took over for me. Their eyes glued to the page, the other students didn't seem to notice the switch in readers.

"'Then one day the boy came to the tree and the tree said, *Come, Boy, come and climb up my trunk and swing from my branches.*'" He read with inflection. He paused at periods and commas. The words magically rolled off his tongue. Our hearts and minds whispered, *Keep going, Miguel Ángel. Please don't stop. We love listening to your voice.* But he stopped eventually—and that was okay too. I read again, picking up the pace slightly. Miguel Ángel and I alternated in this natural flow for the twelve pages of the book.

When we reached the last line, students turned the page expecting more. They didn't want the story to end.

Miguel Ángel allowed me little time to savor my students' success. Already at the controls, he searched YouTube for *The Giving Tree* video. Once again, I fell victim to his speed, grace, and charm. The class sat in a circle on beanbags in eager anticipation. A row of perfect angels, I could find no reason to withhold their reward.

The identical illustrations from Silverstein's book splashed across the white screen. Their enlarged size made them more appealing. The title, too, appeared in oversized letters, making the reading accessible. *How great*, I thought. *What could go wrong with this short, innocent cartoon? It will give perfect closure to a memorable lesson.* Miguel Ángel, his finger poised to click the mouse, looked at me imploringly.

"Okay," I surrendered. But the familiar mischievous grin on his face should have made me question whether he was being an *ángel* or a *diablo*.

Like Geppetto's Pinocchio, the small boy in the book miraculously came to life and his long legs pranced in bended arcs across the screen. Next, the tree, mouthing the words, befriended the boy. The cartoon followed the text verbatim. I relaxed in the knowledge that the story my students had just read would now be revisited, giving them a chance to unscramble some of the vocabulary jumbled in their brains.

Then everything changed. The cartoon was now deviating from the story line. Instead of sitting under the tree to ponder nature, the boy grabbed an axe and angrily shouted, "I don't want your fucking apples." He chopped the tree to pieces, spewing vulgarities with each strike. I scanned the students' faces for signs of distress. The shift in plot happened so abruptly that it might not have registered yet. But the kid in charge had anticipated the scene and was rolling on the floor laughing. My bulging eyes and dropped jaw must have been a sight.

I quickly paused the video before we witnessed more violence to the tree.

"Miss Smit," he said, gasping for air, "I tol' you the video was the same like the book and you believe me. Ha ha. But is really a little bit the same."

I downplayed the situation. "Yes, you fooled me. I should have watched it myself before I let you show it to the class. It's my fault."

"I fool you," he bragged, pointing his finger and giving me a sideways wink. He lifted himself back onto his beanbag.

Suddenly it was my turn to laugh at the ridiculousness of the situation. Following my lead, the students let loose, cracking up, covering mouths—a bonding moment. Then I was saved by the bell.

"Miguel Ángel! Again? No!" students often shouted in utter annoyance. They'd drop their heads onto their desks, knowing from past experience that the gridlock would last several minutes while the class techie reconnected whatever cable was causing the problem—the one he'd purposely disconnected. Other times a lesson came to a halt until he begrudgingly retrieved, at his classmates' insistence, the mouse he'd intentionally hidden that belonged with my teaching computer.

My students' tolerance for his inappropriateness impressed me. More mature students overlooked him. Less mature students seldom got angry, and when they did, they moved away from him, or shouted at him, or in rare instances punched him. Miguel Ángel relentlessly badgered kids—for a pencil, a dollar—and taunted them for how they smelled. I assumed that he got away with what he did because of his small size. But I also secretly suspected that, like me, the kids had a soft spot for him.

The number of disruptions he caused grew right along with his body. In sixth grade, whenever he had a run-in with a teacher or a scuffle with a student, the administration sent him to my classroom for a "cooling off" period. They believed we had a strong bond. By eighth grade, though, our rapport had fundamentally changed. I went from being the teacher he most trusted to the teacher who most disappointed him. Because of the longevity of our relationship, three consecutive years for ninety minutes a day, he'd come to relate to me as a parent—an unpopular role in an adolescent's life. My soft spot for him didn't help matters. I tried to be consistent, less lenient, but I didn't always succeed.

When Miguel Ángel demonstrated good conduct or grades, he received rewards in my classroom and through other school-wide incentive programs. He earned video game time, ice cream parties, pizza, prizes, invitations to extracurricular movies and trips. Communities in Schools, a campus-based dropout prevention program, worked with him by providing a mentor. Eventually he received special education services.

Yet despite positive reinforcement and support, Miguel Ángel continued to accumulate school suspensions for fighting with or threatening peers, using the computer inappropriately, and destroying school property. He frequented the in-school referral center for infractions such as skipping class or insubordination. He spent six weeks in an alternative learning environment, removed from campus. No consequence, positive or negative, produced a major behavioral shift.

With time, the insubordination became a daily occurrence. When asked to move his seat or stop talking, he refused. He openly cursed and verbally abused anyone who confronted him. "You can't do nothing to me. What you gonna do? Ha," he'd retort. I'd have to call for the assistant principal or security guard to remove him. Even *they* struggled with him. What was worse, their goading and threatening squandered precious instructional time.

Miguel Ángel's behavior was now exacerbating students, teachers, administrators, and his parents. Kids who present severe discipline problems at school often experience minimal parenting and an absent father. Not Miguel Ángel. Both his mother and father participated in his school life and showed genuine concern. Driven to school in a shiny Lexus, he was sometimes accompanied by one or both parents into my portable.

His mother's energy trumped whatever else was going on the minute she entered. A Cruella De Vil come to life, she strutted through the door dressed in leopard-print tights, high heels, glittery gold rings on all fingers, and a stunning long-haired wig. She greeted me European-style, a gentle peck on each cheek.

"Maestra, ¿cómo se comporta mi hijo?" Mrs. Morales inquired about her son's behavior in a booming, exuberant voice. I tried to stay positive. When I gave favorable feedback, she blew a kiss to the air or, worse, grabbed Miguel Ángel and gave him a noisy smooch on his forehead in front of his friends. Hearing unfavorable feedback, she feigned shock and disbelief and wailed his name. Yet he behaved the same with or without her in the room, gravitating to the computers and his friends, holding some form of electronic device.

Miguel Ángel's father also commanded a strong presence, despite his soft-spoken manner. Rumor had it that he'd been a professional boxer in Cuba. For a brief time, he taught boxing in the after-school program at our school, where, even in the company of the imposing figure of his own father, Miguel Ángel would misbehave enough to be seen standing outside the locked door of the boxing session.

One of my more creative endeavors to get the little troublemaker to behave involved inviting his father to shadow him for an entire day. I hoped he would suffer enough shame and embarrassment from his dad being at his side that I could use it as leverage. I imagined later threatening Miguel Ángel: *Do we need to get your father up here for another day?* In my fantasy, he'd immediately respond with a vigorous *no!*

Open to any suggestions that could help his troubled son, Mr. Morales entered my class on the appointed day, several steps behind Miguel Ángel. He barely fit his massive body into a student seat. As the morning dragged on, with Mr. Morales observing my every move as well as his son's, I felt like my teaching was being critiqued. The awkward arrangement didn't bear repeating. And besides, Miguel Ángel's behavior had only meagerly improved. He hadn't conducted himself like the "perfect angel" I'd hoped for, although he did—slightly—temper his negative attitude.

Throughout all their time spent anguishing over Miguel Ángel, his parents never seemed to get angry. But another student, Edwin, once disclosed having seen the father smash his son's cell phone against the brick wall that faced the portable. I was probably responsible. During an impromptu meeting after school with both of them, I'd suggested taking Miguel Ángel's phone away for a week as punishment for things like playing on it instead of doing schoolwork. "Miss Smit, you shouldn't of tol' that to the dad of Miguel Ángel," Edwin scolded me. "When he dad come outside yesterday, he say to Miguel Ángel, 'Take away your phone, ha. That's not all I gonna do.' He dad got so mad he crack the phone with his hand and throw it to the wall." This news surprised me. I didn't recall Miguel Ángel without a phone. Of course, the father, regretting his action, might have bought him a replacement that same afternoon.

I detected among many parents a subtle hesitance over punishing their children. New to this country, they didn't feel informed about the cultural expectations of child-rearing here. At times, parents admitted to a reluctance to set boundaries with their children because they felt threatened by agencies such as Child Protective Services. They feared entanglements with the law because of their illegal status.

My students could, and did, take advantage of their parents' uncertainty. With youth on their side, kids learned English and acclimated faster in their new country. The parents depended on them to relay information during visits to the doctor's office, counselor's office, or any number of official agencies. The kids might not have always resisted the urge to censor what didn't suit their personal interests, or they might have preyed on their parents' fears by exaggerating or intentionally misinforming them.

I sensed too that refugee and immigrant parents looked for ways to compensate their children for having experienced emotional upheaval, trauma, and violence early in life. Case in point: Miguel Ángel. He'd brought lots of emotional baggage from Cuba, according to what his mother gradually and sporadically divulged to school personnel. He'd survived a house fire in Cuba. He'd watched his father physically dragged off to prison, where he remained for many months. Several of his extended male family members were still in Cuban prisons. And in a detention center while waiting to enter the United States, the Morales family had witnessed violence firsthand. Throughout, and despite, all the chaos in their lives, the mother had kept intact all the documentation of her son's psychiatric intervention in Cuba and his medical prescriptions.

Immigrant or not, Miguel Ángel's profile and the host of problems involved in educating him were not uncommon. There are scores of Miguel Ángels in American public schools, particularly with regard to their suffering from combinations of parent incarceration, post-traumatic stress, and dyslexia and other learning disabilities. The delayed entry of immigrant youth into public school can have the effect of compounding their problems due to late diagnoses, or, even worse, no diagnosis at all. Miguel Ángel became identified as a special education student in eighth grade, three and a half years after his entry date.

I believe his ultimate saving grace was his ability to relate to other people's struggles. And in moments and situations when I least expected it, when his classmates appeared to be unmoved, he would reveal a very sensitive, compassionate side. Take, for example, his reaction to—of all things—a 1962 movie.

Reading any lengthy text proved arduous for kids acquiring English. I often resorted to abridged versions. To break up the monotony of reading a novel in which many students comprehended 50 percent of the vocabulary at most, I would rent the movie counterpart on video. *Oliver Twist, Holes, A Christmas Carol, Huckleberry Finn, The Elephant Man, Robinson Crusoe, The Wizard of Oz*—all of these I showed in my classroom because they corresponded well with the novels.

Movies, because of their visual nature, reinforced comprehension if they tracked the novel's story line closely. They also provided an incentive. I insisted that students complete a chapter or certain segment of text before viewing the parallel part of the movie. After following this routine for a few rounds, the students would be hooked, though not necessarily on the book. They grew eager to read the next part so they could get back to the movie.

During Miguel Ángel's seventh-grade year, the standard core curriculum for language arts designated "biography" as a six-week unit. I didn't always comply with the core curriculum, particularly when it didn't serve students new to English. Yet for the biography unit, I felt inclined to do so because I had the perfect movie in mind: *The Miracle Worker.* The story of Annie Sullivan and Helen Keller was one of my personal all-time favorites. My preteen students would especially enjoy the dramatic dining room scene, in which actors Anne Bancroft and Patty Duke battle over table manners. Annie makes several attempts to physically force Helen to eat with a spoon. Each time Annie succeeds, Helen spits a mouthful of food in Annie's face. *Every middle school student fantasizes about spitting in some teacher's face*, I thought. I also figured that the water pump scene might resonate with my class. In it, Helen makes the critical connection that the liquid running down her hand has a name, and, therefore, everything does. I could imagine ESL learners easily relating to someone trying to acquire language at its basic level. So, I persevered with my idea. Luckily, I had to look no further than the school library for an "easy reader" book about Annie Sullivan. It contained sixty pages with large print and was at a fourth-grade reading level. Still a challenge, but manageable.

The morning arrived for me to introduce the book. The class stared blankly as I made my pitch for Annie Sullivan. I knew their enthusiasm for the story would build over time, but I needed at least a mild interest out of the gate.

Rumblings of protest sounded from the back of the room. "Who this teacher lady Annie?" Miguel Ángel moaned. "Why we have to read 'bout her? Just 'cause she has a name like you? Ann? Let's read 'bout Fidel. Yeah. Come on. Someone famous from *our* country." Leave it to Miguel Ángel to take aim at my self-reproach for picking a white American who lived over 150 years ago. He continued his scornful remarks, calling out random suggestions, mostly famous Cuban boxers or athletes.

The students grew tired of his complaining. "Miguel Ángel, stop!" Magaly yelled. "Let Miss Smit teach us. You don't know everything. You bothering me."

"Yeah, shut up," Magaly's friend Josefina chimed in. I counted on strong personalities to subdue him.

My rational mind revisited the drawbacks to my choice, which Miguel Ángel had alluded to. One, cultural insensitivity. Two, very traditional. And three, too much of a disconnect. Yet my inner voice persisted. The handicaps

Helen Keller overcame, aided by her teacher, made for an invaluable story for young people who faced obstacles themselves. So what if she led the conventional list of prominent American heroes. Studying history and culture came with the territory of learning a foreign language.

The initial chapters of a book for any reader can be tedious. Familiarizing yourself with the setting and the characters takes work. All this new information, along with the issues of limited background knowledge and language, usually proved overwhelming for ESL students. The opening chapters of the easy reader on Annie Sullivan included extraneous detailed descriptions. The early scenes of the movie version corresponded to the book's first chapters, yet they incorporated flashbacks that made the movie hard to follow. To avoid my students' getting bogged down from the get-go in a nonessential part of the plot, I hurriedly read aloud the opening chapter, delving very little into its content. Eyes drooped, heads rested on elbows, and the tapping of pencils on table edges dinged from spots around the classroom. Desperate not to lose anyone, I coached them through retelling a paragraph in their own words, which I wrote verbatim on the board. They then copied it in their notebooks. Copying tended to keep students focused, provided I didn't overuse it.

In the midst of all my angst over the students' resistance and disinterest, the event a public schoolteacher fears most took place: a surprise administrative observation. On this morning of the biography's introduction, Ms. Price, the principal, had decided to visit my classroom in search of active student engagement and academic rigor—neither of which existed. After silently turning her master key in the lock, she stepped inside and tiptoed to an empty chair next to, of all students, Miguel Ángel. She slithered into the seat, a snake avoiding detection. Her eyes narrowed at the list of lesson objectives displayed on the blackboard, which she copied onto her standard yellow checklist. Once apprised of those objectives, she glanced left and right, taking note of the students, their actions and expressions.

Initially none of them noticed the principal, except for Miguel Ángel. Sensing an opportunity to interject since the lesson was obviously not flowing, he started in again on his litany of rappers, athletes, and other famous Cubans who he thought made good subjects for a biography. Luckily for me, the class ignored him, and soon he turned to mumbling and whining for the benefit of those within earshot—namely, the principal. Watching him from the corner of my eye felt like watching a ship sink in slow motion. Unable to do anything to change the course of events, I stopped myself from looking in his direction. I'd deal with the aftermath later.

Then, once again, luck was with me. The students rallied. Slumped shoulders straightened. Hands shot up in the air. Fingers traced lines of text as mouths silently formed the words. I wondered how they knew to perform on cue. But it didn't matter, since I was facing a barrage of eager responses.

"The writer suggests," I said, "that Annie, like Helen Keller, can't see very well. What sentence on page five tells us that Annie can't see well? Read to the class the one sentence on page five that explains that Annie can't see." I posed the question twice, varying the vocabulary to bolster comprehension.

Alex, excited to participate, didn't wait for me to recognize him and began stumbling through a long sentence that had nothing to do with poor eyesight.

"Well, Alex, that sentence is talking about Annie," I said. "But not about her eyes. What do people put in front of their eyes to see?" I hinted.

"Glasses," Miguel Ángel shouted instantly. His copy of the book lay on the floor, but he was tuned into the discussion. "This is too easy. Too dumb. Let's read something else." He'd seized another chance to disrupt.

I quickly moved on. "Maybe you've found the sentence," I said to Thida, who was waving her hand frantically in the air after hearing the "glasses" cue. She read the part describing Annie's near blindness, which mentioned that the teacher wore thick glasses.

"That's exactly it. Perfect," I practically shrieked. The thumbs-up I gave Thida made her beam.

The observation lasted a painful twenty minutes. On her way out, Ms. Price left the yellow checklist on top of a heap of papers on my desk. At lunch I skimmed the items checked and unchecked, as well as the notes written in the form's margins.

> *Most students engaged*
> *Teacher prompts appropriately*
> *Students actively reading*
> *Students searching for text evidence*

I breathed a sigh of relief. Not bad. She'd been generous.

But there was one note that hurt: *Why Annie Sullivan?* It glared at me from the form's final section, titled "Wonderings." And it signaled that Miguel Ángel had steered others—important, power-wielding others—to doubt what I too had earlier doubted. The creators of the form had included that last section to prompt teachers to self-reflect. Yet I had reflected plenty. I stood firm with *The Miracle Worker.*

Two weeks into the biography, kids were rushing to class so as to ensure their allotted movie time. For every lesson they had to do forty minutes of reading aloud, fluency practice passages, cloze passages, grammar drills, vocabulary building games, question-and-answer discussions, or writing short narratives that related to the story. After that, I rewarded them with the next part of the movie.

Each day Miguel Ángel, having long forgotten his disdain for Annie Sullivan, scurried to the computer to display the movie on the large screen. "Please, everyone. We got only twelve minute," he would announce. "Miss Smit not going to let us watch till everyone is quiet. Dang, why you take so long?" No one protested his bossiness as they shuffled chairs and beanbags into comfortable positions. I think they were as pleased as I was by his change in attitude.

The students would settle down. A hush would fall over the room. After Miguel Ángel clicked "play," the movie would pick up where it had stopped the previous day. Then he'd dive into a beanbag that practically had his name on it. The first time I'd showed it, everyone had groaned at the black-and-white images and exclaimed how "really, really old" the movie was. Now they hardly noticed its outdated appearance.

On a Friday afternoon we reached the pivotal scene, the one I'd eagerly awaited during the last two weeks—the water pump scene. Helen breaks away from her teacher, runs across the yard, and grabs the handle of the pump. When water gushes out, she lets go and the water trickles down her fingers. Her eyes toward the sky, her mouth wide open, she freezes in an epiphany: water has a name! The hand movements she and Annie Sullivan had practiced all those months weren't silly games but a means of referencing things. Helen immediately starts banging on objects around her—the ground, the pump, the tree—and demanding to know what they're called. Annie signs the words into her hand.

Curious whether the kids were tearing up like I was, I glanced around the dimly lit classroom. My eyes traveled from profile to profile, seeing their gazes riveted to the shadowy screen. Unaware of my spying, nobody moved or made a sound.

My search eventually came to rest on Miguel Ángel. His huge eyes stared ahead. Fat tears rolled down his cheeks.

I couldn't help myself. My one chance to get back at him from our last video fiasco. My turn to misbehave. "Miguel Ángel," I said, feigning surprise, "are you crying?"

His reaction, however, *did* surprise me. "Yeah," he conceded softly, not turning his head. He remained mesmerized by what he'd just witnessed. "I think that white girl [Patty Duke], she kind of pretty," he added unashamedly. He was completely captivated by *The Miracle Worker.* All my students were. The bell sounded. Instead of bursting out the door piled on top of one another as usual, they exited unrushed, as if in a trance.

I felt overjoyed whenever students immersed themselves in a story. To this day, I remain grateful that my intuition prevailed over a few others' opinions on the selection of the Annie Sullivan biography. I sensed that Helen Keller's story would particularly resonate with my ESL learners, and it did.

To be fair, Miguel Ángel was, at times, an asset to a class, not only because he rallied students but also because his energy and curiosity fueled my creativity. Ultimately, though, he and students like him depleted me. I started to feel that my job description had changed without notification, my teaching duties usurped by counseling and policing demands. I resented the extra non-class time I spent to rescue Miguel Ángel: writing reports, documenting disruptive behavior and poor academic performance, meeting with his parents, meeting with the social worker and school counselors, meeting with his other teachers, meeting with him—time I could have allocated to planning quality instruction, which I considered my main job.

The minutes that led to hours coaxing Miguel Ángel to stay on task, or simply not to disrupt, was time lost serving other students who needed assistance and were receptive to learning and achieving. The missed opportunities to help others progress—especially those who tended not to make waves—proved to be a root cause of my stress.

During the tumultuous Miguel Ángel years, I heard a remark made by the legendary Texas musician and politician, Kinky Friedman, that has always stuck with me. In a radio interview during his campaign for governor, he said, "What happened to no *teacher* left behind?"

My thoughts exactly.

Juan (AKA Yawn)

"You know what the kids call you, don't you?" my new colleague, Sonia Cruz, baited me as we lesson-planned over coffee and donuts from the 7-Eleven.

"They just call me Miss Smith, as best they can pronounce it." Then I realized what she was insinuating. "You mean they have a nickname for me too?" I asked, my eyes widening.

"Of course," Sonia ribbed. "What do you mean *for me too*?" Her ability to relate and understand nuances of the Mexican culture gave her an advantage. Raised in the Texas border city of McAllen, Sonia was bilingual and bicultural, whereas I was from Hartford, Connecticut, and neither the former nor the latter.

"They call you Látigo," Sonia informed me, popping a piece of donut into her mouth. "A *látigo* is a long whip." She wore a mischievous smile, as if she knew what I would say next.

"Oh. They call me Látigo because of how I can *whip* everybody into shape," I declared, aware of speaking with more certainty than I felt. I yearned to be a master disciplinarian.

Sonia nearly choked on a sip of coffee. "No, silly.

They call you Látigo because you're long and skinny like a whip."

I knew that nicknames in this Mexican tradition were meant to be affectionate yet not necessarily flattering. In many cases they were based on a perceived physical or character flaw. During my teaching years I heard, among others, Feo (Ugly), Gordo (Fatty), Loco (Crazy), Chata (Pug Nose), and Flaca (Skinny). I decided to appreciate that I was assigned one at all, regardless of its meaning or basis.

Now that Sonia was working alongside me, I had an insider's take on private jokes and innuendos that circulated among the students. Sonia took the humor a step further. Not only did she come up with quirky names for students herself, but she also had the artistic talent to create on-demand cartoon sketches of people, objects, and scenes. The kids got a kick out of them. Here's one she drew of me trying to stay awake at a staff meeting. (I've kept it all these years.)

It was Sonia who gave our student Juan his pet name "Yawn." Juan was an eighth-grader who had arrived at our school as green as they come. He didn't speak a word of English. And the fact that he entered the U.S. school system later in the year further undermined his ability to learn on an equal playing field.

Blessed with angular features and a square jaw, his good looks offset his nerdish mannerisms. So great was his passion and drive to understand and communicate that his eyes and ears seemed to pulsate with deliberation. His gaze never wavered from me—my hand signals, my writing on the board, my words. I was the orchestra conductor, he the musician. I felt like a human lifeline to invaluable information.

I first noticed Juan's extreme attentiveness during a vocabulary activity called Concentration, a modified version of the well-known card game. One by one, students approached the blackboard and turned over two pieces of paper from an array of them taped facedown. If the chosen two revealed a match—for example, an antonym pair—the student kept those two papers and continued playing. Not locating a match meant the student turned the two papers back over and returned to their seat. Later, students redeemed their matches for a prize of some sort.

On my day of revelation about Juan, Concentration was taking too long. I'd included an overabundance of matches, and the necessary recall proved too difficult. To have to remember the location of a word, its meaning, its opposite, and the location of its opposite was overwhelming the kids. They gradually disengaged, all except Juan. His eyes darted from paper to paper, taking in every detail while the others held side conversations and asked to go to the restroom.

When Carmen, a student more concerned with her pretty looks than her intellect, got to the blackboard, instead of turning over only two of the papers, she tried to ruin the game by revealing all the words one by one, laughing as she did so. At this point I decided to cut the game short. But as I peeled off the first taped paper from the board, Juan's determined expression and tense facial muscles somehow caught my attention. I could not disappoint.

"Juan, do you want to try?" I offered, shushing the class. He immediately looked away, then down at his feet, up at the ceiling, and finally at me. He wore a bashful grin, which told me he welcomed the opportunity. With students growing more restless by the second, I needed to rein them in before losing them completely. But I hated to rush Juan, well aware of the courage it took to perform in front of peers he barely knew. I motioned Juan to come to the board, and luckily he did.

He proceeded to uncover matches like a blind person reading Braille. With eyes shut, he dragged his hand vertically from paper to paper. At each one he'd pause as if tracing the letters.

"Hey, Miss. He cheating. He look too close and see to the other side," someone yelled.

But I wasn't so sure. Juan's heavy lids covered most of his eyes. Also, I inspected a paper for myself to see if the marker I'd used to create the game had bled through. But not even I could make out the letters—and I had written the words.

Juan's first successful antonym match of *black/white* seemed credible. Language learners, especially young ones, memorize colors and numbers first. The next two matches were also plausible. *Day/night* are common vocabulary words; in addition, *day* and *día* are cognates, that is, words from two languages similar in meaning, spelling and, to a certain degree, pronunciation. *Funny/serious* followed— less basic vocabulary, but *serious* and *serio* are cognates too.

The students' annoying chatter subsided. Juan had gotten their attention. Eight papers remained taped to the board. Four matches. Juan took a step backward and surveyed their positions. He rubbed the fingers of one hand across his stubbly chin, a chess player contemplating his next move. The following pair of antonyms he put together wasn't so plausible. *Cheap/expensive* share no cognates in Spanish and are difficult even to pronounce. Still six papers left. *Dangerous/safe* followed, then *full/empty*, and finally *strong/weak*. Juan was unstoppable. The board now showing a clean slate, he faced the class and grinned sheepishly.

"Way to go, Juan! You got them all!" I cheered, clapping and hooting. None of the students joined in, maybe from disbelief. Juan gravitated to his seat.

A similar scenario with Juan played out repeatedly. He would refrain from participating until clearly no one else could perform the task. Then, when prompted by me, and initially with reluctance, he'd never fail to identify the correct response, pattern, or sequence of words. His capacity to retain information floored me. Eventually, I attributed Juan's success to either a photographic memory or a keen intelligence, if not genius. Maybe both. Seemingly modest by nature, he insisted on being unobtrusive. I tried to honor that by restraining my excitement or delight whenever he delivered the solution.

I started to notice that in his moments just prior to volunteering, as if in hesitation Juan would habitually turn his head toward a shoulder. The gesture was so subtle I thought I imagined it. Then he'd mysteriously wipe his mouth on a sleeve as if hiding something. Like a magician concealing the ace of spades. I simply couldn't understand why he did this. After seeing him do the same thing a dozen times, though, I began to suspect that he was yawning. And yet he didn't appear to be tired or bored, but rather the opposite—intensely engaged.

One afternoon my colleague Sonia confirmed my suspicion. She stood next to me in my portable, and the two of us watched Juan work his magic. "We should call him 'Yawn,'" she whispered. And we did. "Yawn" became our code name for him from that point on.

Only much later did I realize that Juan's yawning might have been a form of social anxiety.

"Ms. Smith, you know our *primo* Juan?" Oscar mumbled to me out of the blue as I reviewed spelling words with him and his sister Teresa. I'd discovered only a few days earlier that they were siblings, even though they'd sat in my classroom the last four months. Now they were divulging another family relationship. Their timing wasn't good—they both struggled with literacy and sorely needed the spelling review time—but I welcomed any chance to connect with them.

"Juan," I repeated. "I teach a dozen Juans. Juan who?"

"Juan Ignacio."

Oscar had supplied the middle name. I assumed he didn't know Juan's last name. "Does he go to school here now?" I asked.

Oscar shook his head. "He suppose to be in high school. You his teacher like maybe four year before." He and his sister went from smiling to giggling, amused that I couldn't remember *their* Juan.

"I remember a Juan Fernando. Is that your cousin? He had reddish hair. Very tall. He was hyper. *Muy activo.*"

"No. Juan Fernando his homeboy. I know Juan Fernando too." Oscar smiled so nonstop that he barely formed words with his lips when he spoke. I often had to guess at what he said.

"What's happening with Juan Fernando? Does he go to Travis [the closest high school]?" I asked.

Again Oscar shook his head. "No. He deliver pizza with Domino's. He have a fast car. New." He raised his eyebrows and nodded with approval. The news about Juan Fernando didn't surprise or disappoint me. I remembered that he had trouble sitting in a chair for any length of time. Driving around South Austin in a flashy vehicle fit his personality.

Suddenly my memory cleared, as if a camera lens had been adjusted. I'd taught Juan Fernando and Juan Ignacio (Yawn) the same year. "What about Juan Ignacio? Does he go to high school?" I dreaded the response.

For the third time Oscar shook his head. "No, Miss.

He can't. He have to work. His family need money. He work at Taco Bell. *Food prep*, he say."

My heart sank, but Oscar held his smile. Teresa too. In their families, a service industry job was a predictable and reliable outcome. "Did he go to high school for two years? Maybe just one year?" I pressed.

Oscar shrugged. Evidently, the tabs he kept on his cousin weren't as close as I'd thought.

In my mind I quickly went over the tenable reasons for Juan having quit school, brilliant as he was. His parents deemed school a low priority, and money talked. Not highly educated themselves, his parents might not have appreciated the value of an education. The school system failed Juan because he'd entered at fifteen, not a common age for children to acquire a designation such as special education or—the category I believed applied to Juan—gifted and talented. I wanted to blame the high school, but it was possible Juan never stepped foot in one if he'd turned sixteen (the legal age to drop out) during the summer between eighth grade and high school. I briefly panicked, wondering if I'd been the one and only adult in Juan's life aware of his capabilities. I'd naively assumed he would stay in school, particularly since he seemed to enjoy it so much.

"He want me tell you hi," offered Oscar, the perpetual grinner.

"Tell Juan Ignacio to come see me," I said, already conjuring a rescue. Not trusting that Juan would show up, I imagined myself knocking on the kitchen door of Taco Bell and convincing him to go back to school. Then, returning to the present moment, I said, "You know, your cousin is really, *really* smart."

Oscar and Teresa looked at me, their expressions unchanged. I couldn't tell if they agreed. I thought about the amazing talent this extended family had generated: Juan Ignacio, a near-genius, and Oscar, a gifted athlete. I'd never met the parents of either boy. I wondered if they had any notion of the potential of their sons. I lived in a community of white privilege where parents spent inordinate amounts of time and money for their kids to become super achievers.

Of all my former students, Juan deserved not only a high school diploma but higher education. Curious, intelligent, passionate, and driven, he possessed the perfect combination for greatness. But he was also an immigrant and poor. I minimized my disappointment by downplaying his situation. His decision to leave school didn't necessarily seal his fate. Not pursuing an education at the conventional age didn't have to prevent him from gaining one later. Many people got their GED and continued on to higher education. I imagined Juan lucky enough to cross paths with a mentor—his Taco Bell manager, for instance. The man would recognize his ambition and intelligence and take him under his wing, shifting Juan's life's trajectory, paying for his education. Possible outcomes, but not probable.

I consciously pushed away the thoughts lingering in a far recess of my mind: maybe Juan, although an avid and devoted student, had realized the enormity of what lay ahead of him. The sheer magnitude of what he'd have to accomplish in four years of high school. And the preposterous challenge of *beginning* to acquire a second language, at an academic level, when he was already fifteen. A high school diploma required passing five academic exams in English—reading, writing, mathematics, science, and history. To go from zero English to receiving a high school diploma in four or five years was no easy feat for any human on the planet. Maybe Juan had simply decided to spare himself the frustration. Such a decision now seemed to me completely understandable, maybe even practical.

"You be sure to tell your cousin Juan Ignacio that Ms. Smith said to come see her," I heard myself tell Oscar and Teresa. I guess I couldn't completely give up on the situation. I had to make one last-ditch effort, for what it was worth.

"I tell him," Oscar good-naturedly assured me. But I questioned Oscar's level of commitment. He could easily forget.

Juan Ignacio (AKA Yawn) never did show up at my portable.

In Defense of Public Education

I couldn't resist peeking out the window as I walked the perimeter of the long table, placing textbooks several inches apart. I wondered if my students' families were making their way to the portable. The wall clock said 6:55 p.m., the designated time for parents to exit the gym and follow their child's abbreviated schedule of classes.

Although not totally ready for this Back to School Night, I felt confident. Student writing covered the two bulletin boards: rudimentary paragraphs titled "My Classmate" accompanied colorful photos of smiling faces. A clipboard by the door contained handouts with my contact information for the parents to conveniently grab. The custodians had spent extra time mopping the discolored linoleum floor and straightening furniture. The yellow and turquoise hues in the craft paper and wall paint throughout the classroom, combined with the fading sunlight, created an inviting ambience. A wall of wooden shelves lined with books and magazines of varying sizes and shapes added to the cozy atmosphere.

I didn't need to be as prepared as other teachers at the school. They followed protocol. They produced a three-page syllabus for parents to peruse, and they wrote a catchy bio to use to introduce themselves. After all, what languages would my materials be translated into? A visitor who entered my portable that evening wasn't likely to speak English but rather one of a variety of other languages.

My resistance to the pomp and circumstance was also linked to low parent turnout. If this Back to School Night was in keeping with the event in years past, a smattering of six or seven parents would pass through the portable, smiling, thanking, asking few questions. I didn't see the practicality of taking time to edit a curriculum for a handful of obliging parents who seemed completely trusting of my ability to educate their children.

A part of me felt grateful not to have to address a large adult audience, yet still a nagging disappointment persisted. Where were my students' parents or guardians this evening? I reminded myself of all the possible reasons for their absence: restaurant and hotel jobs that required evening shifts, caring for younger children at home, sheer fatigue, the intimidation of an academic institution, the language barrier, fear of the authorities discovering their immigration status. And then some students didn't live with their parents but rather with older *hermanos, cuñadas, tíos* or *tías*—siblings, sisters-in-law, aunts or uncles—while their parents remained in their country of origin.

Year after year, on Back to School Night (ironically—for me at least—also called Meet the Teacher Night) I sat alone in my portable, which was separate from the main buildings, awaiting visitors. I was a wallflower at a school dance, or Cinderella feeling out of place at the prince's ball.

Peering out the window one last time, I wavered between emotions of anticipation and doubt. Aha! Three people were standing outside my door, having seemingly materialized out of nowhere. I recognized my student Lifen, who for some unknown reason we called Amy. From Beijing, Amy was one of only two students I'd ever taught who had entered American schools as a highly advanced math student. She was also a standout member of the choir. In

204

other words, Amy didn't fit the standard profile of students assigned to me. And just then I realized that neither did her parents. They huddled together, looking at a printout of Amy's schedule. I quickly popped open my door and waved them in.

The man stormed through the entryway, Amy and her Chinese mother trailing behind. "There's a problem here!" he barked. The door banged behind him. A heavy textbook crashed to the floor when he slammed his briefcase on the table. "Two weeks into the school year and Lifen's *still* not in her correct math class. Everything being taught in the class she's now in she learned five years ago in China. Her time's being wasted. It's ridiculous how far behind American students are compared to Chinese students."

Since the man was Anglo and ranting in perfect English, I assumed he was Amy's stepfather. Amy and her mom appeared to form an alliance with each other by keeping a wide distance from him.

Caught off guard, I felt myself lifted out of a slight haze into a situation where I needed to execute an immediate, tactful reply. But I had little practice dealing with angry parents in any language, English included. Up until this moment, parents for the most part had been a non-factor. Now, so unexpectedly, here stood a man demanding answers from *me*.

Various responses, either too disparaging or too blunt, went through my head. I refused to make his concern of a *schedule adjustment* bigger than it needed to be.

He continued to spout his outrage over the failings of our school and, more broadly, American public education. Meanwhile, a couple entered and seated themselves at a table. Surprisingly, they showed no reaction to the stepfather's tirade.

Time to take charge, I told myself.

"Can we talk about Amy's math class in a few minutes?" I interrupted. "These parents have come to hear about their child's first-period ESL class. Amy doesn't have my class until fourth period. And right now it's only first period, according to tonight's program." I glanced toward the seated pair. For the first time, the stepfather took note of his surroundings. He gave the other parents an apologetic nod and stepped away from the table to join Amy and her mom. Relieved that I'd managed to buy some time, I turned my back to him.

A third, fourth, then fifth adult slipped in and joined the couple at the table. With each new arrival, my motivation to conduct a presentation grew. I made it a point to begin promptly since my session with them lasted only ten minutes. Fortunately, all of the more recent arrivals spoke exclusively Spanish, so making the decision to employ my own limited Spanish was a no-brainer.

"En primer lugar, esta clase es la más importante de su hijo o hija. En esta clase aprenderá inglés." I always began by explaining to the parents that my class was their child's most important one since it was where they would learn English. I noticed chins dipping and eyes blinking. Signs of acknowledgment.

Next, I held up the Spanish-English dictionary I'd ordered at the beginning of the year for each newly enrolled ESL student. *"Este libro, un diccionario, es el mejor amigo de su hijo o hija durante el año escolar."* This dictionary would be their child's best friend during the school year, I told them. Then I encouraged the parents to make sure their child took it with them wherever they went. Granted, this was an exaggeration; but I wanted to emphasize that effort and discipline were needed to learn English.

After describing a daily lesson and the overall academic goals, I couldn't resist ending on a note of urgency: ninety minutes a day wasn't an adequate amount of time to acquire a second language, and their kids really needed to watch TV in English and read in English at home as much as possible.

Handshakes and pleasantries followed. In my presentation, this is when I would comment on individual students.

"Efren es adorable," I said of the first couple's child, purposefully employing a cognate to make sure I'd used an appropriate word to describe their son. In truth, Efren really was precious and a joy to teach; but by this time I was brain-dead from the pressure of speaking Spanish, my barely second language. I reverted to English. "And look at his good work. He is writing in English already." I beckoned them to the bulletin board to view Efren's paragraph and the photo of his face, which sported an ear-to-ear grin.

Touched, the mom reached up and gave me a hug. *"Muchas gracias, maestra,"* she said. Behind her, the husband gave a thumbs-up, beaming with pride.

The bell sounded and, adhering to the rules, five parents promptly filed out. I noted how their gestures of appreciation had shifted my frame of mind. I felt calmer as I refocused on Amy's family. Still congregated off to the side, they waited for my attention.

"Come sit at the table," I offered. We were the only people in the room. They acted as if they hadn't heard me and remained standing.

"My husband, David," Amy's mother began, "he upset because Lifen have wrong math class. It too easy for her. She finish homework in like five minutes." Amy's hand quickly shot up to suppress her giggling.

"What's so funny, Amy?" I asked.

"My mom. Her English," she said between breaths. "I never listen her English. It sound so funny."

The mom tapped the daughter on the shoulder. "Lifen, this serious. We talking about school problem with your teacher," she scolded softly.

The husband upstaged the wife's gentle demeanor. "Why does moving her into the honors math class have to be this hard?" he demanded. "I told the counselor the day I enrolled Lifen—that's over a month ago—to be sure he put my daughter in the eighth-grade honors math class." (Amy was in seventh grade.) "He must've forgotten. So I've called twice and left messages both times." The husband grimaced. "The class she's in now is a joke."

The word *joke* put me on the defensive. I resented parents who were clueless as to what was involved in running a school and creating over a thousand custom-made schedules. Chances were, the honors math class was held at the same time the choir practiced or Amy's ESL class met— courses she also needed.

The complaint seemed minor. Yes, Amy had endured an unchallenging class for a couple of weeks, but other students of mine suffered through electives way over their heads for an entire semester. I had students with zero English enrolled in a government course offered through the magnet program because it was the only elective available that fit their schedules. Too many ESL students sat in language-heavy electives in which they gained nothing but frustration. Kids who were bombarded for a good portion of their school day by a basically incomprehensible language deserved a break from the constant chatter. A hands-on elective such as art, wood shop, keyboarding, or a choir class would have given them the perfect reprieve, but these classes filled up quickly. My students' time-wasting situation felt more preposterous than Amy's, and yet no adult championed *their* cause. No one was demanding, for example, that the school provide additional art or wood shop classes so my students could get in them.

I tried to let go of my personal resentment and address the issue now before me. I focused on persuading myself of its validity. "There's probably a good reason why Amy hasn't been switched to that math class," I began. "For instance, it might conflict with one of her other classes. I'm sorry no one has explained this to you or to her." I glanced at Amy practicing Cat's Cradle with yarn I'd given her earlier in the week. She didn't appear the least concerned. "But," I continued, "the counselors are very busy this time of year."

"They've had two weeks," David yelled, ironically forming the peace sign with his fingers. I wanted to reply, *Three counselors, one thousand students.* But I held my tongue.

"I don't understand why schools here in America are so behind. And so disorganized." He shook his head. "Really, it's pitiful."

Without thinking, I put my hands on my hips. "Well, maybe it's that Americans are altruistic. We aim to educate everyone, regardless of background. I don't think China does that. Not even Europe does it to the same degree. If you aim for quantity, then sometimes quality suffers." I heard my own voice, hardly recognizing it, not at all certain of the correctness of my words. I was operating on a hunch. The damage done, I braced myself for a torrent of rebukes. None came.

Taking advantage of David's reticence, I pressed on. "I seriously doubt that in China *every* child attends school. China doesn't educate the masses like we do." Pure speculation on my part.

"Well, that's . . . that's probably true," he faltered.

Emboldened, I forged ahead. "It's my understanding that even in Europe, kids from a young age are tracked for either university or a trade school—decisions based on early performance or maybe family background. Here in the United States we resist tracking students. It's an unpopular notion." I paused to give him a chance to speak. Silence. "Here, we try not to continually lump kids together who score within certain ranges on standardized exams. That's just one example. And if we do lump them together, we don't like to admit it. We hold fast to the ideal not to limit any child from any branch of knowledge. The world is their oyster, so to speak. And, just so you know, both scheduling and teaching become really complicated when students aren't grouped according to performance."

By this time, he was teetering on the verge of acquiescence. "I guess I can see your point," he said, making eye contact with me for the first time.

We exchanged one or two other ideas on the matter—and that was the end of it. My last statement to David was my promise to talk with the counselor in the morning about Amy's math situation.

Only later did I learn that Amy's stepfather had a reputation as a vocal, if not outright belligerent, parent who made his presence known every Friday at the weekly parent coffee. If I'd known this fact on that Back to School Night, I would have avoided our conversation. Instead, I spoke my truth and wasn't disregarded by him, or even reprimanded later by my principal.

Schools come under heavy criticism and pressure, which, as a teacher, I certainly took on. The overriding message that schools can close the achievement gap on their own weighs heavy on teachers' shoulders. And when that impossible expectation isn't met, we feel responsible. I believe that most public educators and administrators do the best they can, and I'm grateful that I took at least one opportunity during my career to articulate this when it was called for.

That night I also experienced, for the first and only time during my teaching career, a parent advocating for a child: Amy. I'm convinced that a correlation existed between her parents' strong backing of their daughter and that daughter's achievements in math, music, and English. Demanding customers often get their way—and so do the parents who threaten to go to the school board. That's how life works. Amy got her honors math class and that was a positive. Yet sometimes the positive exposes the negative. Other students suffered through senseless, impractical courses semester after semester.

On that Back to School Night, my eyes were opened

to what students lacked when they didn't have an adult supporting them. Besides the challenge of narrowing the achievement gap, public schools—as the great equalizer—must also serve as a voice for the voiceless.

The Candy Store

A few blocks from the portable where I taught during the last years of my career stood a classic American candy shop. It occupied a storefront on South Congress, an avenue lined with trendy establishments, located up the hill from the Texas State Capitol and the Colorado River. *What teacher wouldn't take advantage of a candy store so close and located on such a well-known block of the state capital?* This is what I'd later justify to myself when considering all the non-instructional class time my students would spend there.

The Big Top Candy Shop served as a decoy. It beckoned. It lured my students and me to walk along the neighborhood streets then glide through its glass doors, bordered by a row of windows streaked with morning sunshine. The reasons for the shop's attraction differed according to age and position in life: its sugary delights, its proximity, the surroundings, the suspense of our being off campus without being caught, taking the hidden alley versus the shadier route, making it back in time so that our whereabouts went unnoticed. Yet for students and teacher, the store meant an adrenaline-rushing, fun-filled adventure.

The first candy store visit took place by happenstance, not design. One sunny autumn afternoon, enjoying the freedom of a pre-approved field trip, my students and I marched single file, chatting and singing, through the tree-lined streets that surrounded our school. Like hikers coming off a narrow, wooded trail, we emerged onto a bright, wide-open clearing—the main avenue. Backpacks bumped up against one another as the kids congregated to receive last-minute instructions.

My students were on assignment: to create maps of the storefronts on either side of the avenue. Soon construction paper, pencils, and rulers appeared from zippered compartments. Clipboards rested on bent knees or a friend's back. Passersby slowed and turned their heads to observe the flurry of activity from children who were supposed to be in school. With fingers pointed and pencils poised, the students embarked on their task. Later, back in the classroom, they'd carry out the next step of that task: to write simple descriptive paragraphs to accompany their maps that would include newly acquired English prepositions and prepositional phrases. But for now the drawings kept them busy—all except the youngest of the group, Manny. He grew tired of most activities quickly, and artwork was no exception. So of course he was the one to discover the candy store.

I eyed him as he wandered several feet from the group to the row of buildings. He inched his way from one window section to the next. Nose touching the glass, he blocked sunlight with his cupped hands to get a view of the interior. Soon his mischievous grin flashed in our direction. He jumped in place and summoned everybody over to the window. "Miss, we can go in? To see the candies?" he pleaded in a high-pitched voice.

The students, now encircling me, echoed Manny. But I wasn't prepared to take twenty of them into a candy store. I tried to reason my way out. "You need money," I countered.

"That's okay. We just want to see," one of them said.

"Please, Miss? Please?" many of them begged.

Carolina foraged through her glittery silver purse then proclaimed, "I have one dollar." She dangled it directly in my field of vision. Her smile melted my resistance. We went inside.

In contrast to the bright sunshine outside, the store's low lighting immediately absorbed us. It was as if we'd entered a dimly lit theater. Everyone grew silent. Spellbound, my students strolled the aisles displaying brand after brand of sweets. On the shelves sat chocolates locked in glass cases and other kinds of candy stocked in rustic wooden boxes. The enchantment of the place was beyond inviting, yet they all managed to keep their wits about them. The bell that marked the end of the school day drew near, and without speaking we headed back to the campus, still in an almost trance-like state. Somewhere along the way, my brain shifted into full gear, creating ways to incorporate into our academic routine this newly discovered treasure.

In the months following that first visit, I maintained the candy store as an addendum to the main part of a field trip—a kind of finale to an excursion to, for instance, the public library, an art museum, or the Texas Capitol. The store, conveniently located on our way back, made willing field trip participants out of kids who didn't get excited about places of educational value.

As might be expected, ultimately the candy store gained center-stage status. Savvier students started to pine for it, even when no field trip loomed on the horizon. One seventh period, a rather studious girl dared to broach the subject. While I was reading a story aloud as everyone followed along, Ana interrupted me. "This book too hard," she moaned. "Let's go the candy store." Not a complainer by nature, she hid her face between bent arms on the table, embarrassed by her outburst. After a slight pause, I continued reading the final paragraph. My words sounded like raindrops on a roof gradually coming to a halt at the end of a downpour . . . and then nothing.

Suddenly Ana's boldness grew contagious. Heads nodded and hands shot up in the air. I shushed the students gently. My subdued response gave me away.

They knew the candy store was a possibility.

"Is so close."

"We walk fast."

"Tomorrow we finish the story."

Everything they'd said was true. The Big Top Candy Shop was close, five minutes tops walking at a fast clip, and the story could wait. Besides, I could also appreciate a diversion.

From that point on, the candy store assumed its rightful status among struggling middle-school learners (and their teacher). It became a frequent reward trip for good behavior and completion of work.

The shop remained a special treat throughout those years for reasons beyond the fact that it offered delicious things to eat. Setting foot inside it always gave me the sensation of stepping back in time. The whole place carried a faint aroma of chocolate combined with the smell of musty, old flooring. I imagined an aging, bearded chocolatier stirring dark syrup in a steaming vat behind the door by the shiny cash register. The background music sounded tinny, as if it came from an antiquated record, a needle moving across its grooves. The store was narrow, giving a sense of an apothecary lined with shelves on either side from floor to ceiling. High above, posters peppered the walls. Faded in color, they advertised obsolete circus shows that featured creepy-looking monkeys and people with various abnormalities. Hung haphazardly beneath the posters were old musical instruments—tarnished trombones and flutes, rusty trumpets with missing valves. Below the instruments was a row of wooden seats attached to each other.

Standing in the midst of all this, I sometimes reflected on the differences in ages and eras that set boundaries between my students and me, and this would bring on a fleeting woefulness for the passage of time. I wondered if my young students were conscious of the outdated nature of the shop, if it seemed in the least strange—after all, some of them were from places in the world that probably hadn't changed much over the years. I hoped they might appreciate its ambience in the same way I did.

The shop brimmed with what appeared to be any type of candy ever marketed. Near the entrance, taffy of every conceivable flavor was arranged in separate barrels low to the ground. The intent was to entice young customers, like my students, who weren't accustomed to seeing multitudes of small items for sale right at their fingertips. At the back stood two sections of bin candies, generally not wrapped and purchased by the pound. These two sections were divided by price, which further complicated logistics. Not only did my students need to familiarize themselves with a scale system, but they also required constant supervision to avoid mixing the differently priced candies together in one bag. I encouraged them to stick to the bins marked "$2.27 per pound." They contained less expensive varieties, including a large assortment of both old and new brands. Lemon Drops. Sweet liquid in mini-wax containers. Charleston Chews. Now & Laters. Bit O' Honey. Hot Tamales. Good & Plenty. Milk Duds. Yet none of these items were given a glance by anyone except me. They were remnants of my childhood only.

I felt a twinge of disappointment each time students approached the scale with the same combinations of Swedish Fish, Gummi Bears, Worms, Skittles, Starbursts, M&M's, Jolly Ranchers, and, of course, bubble gum. I wanted them to be more adventuresome. "You can buy any of these at a 7-Eleven. Try something different," I would say.

Unlike an officially sanctioned field trip, most of our candy store trips were last-minute. Students never knew with certainty if they'd get to go until the actual moment. In this way, I could squeeze every bit of effort from them. I dangled the possibility of the store over their heads, like a dog owner holding a treat just out of the pet's reach. On any given Wednesday, someone excited by the prospect of an outing would mention the potential excursion: "Miss, we can go to the candy store Friday?"

"We'll have to see how it goes," I'd answer, raising my eyebrows to indicate it was under consideration. "It depends on how much work we get done." The suspense of not knowing enhanced the thrill of the game.

On Fridays, students paid special attention to the clock. Yet they knew not to mention the candy store before 10:45. If they pestered me, I could use that as a reason to postpone the visit another week. It opened at 11:00, more or less, and our class ended at 11:25. That gave us roughly twenty-five minutes to get there, select, weigh, and purchase candy, and return in time for the next class period. (And of course there was that extra five minutes of passing time between classes that provided us a bit more leeway on the other end.) So we had our candy store dash down to twenty-five minutes. Twenty-seven in a pinch.

Eyeing the clock, I'd barter with the class—something like this: "If you want to go to the candy store today, you have to finish the next three questions in three minutes. You can all work together." Then the energy would shift. The confident students would reposition their chairs and simultaneously read the questions to themselves, their heads bobbing along with the text, and raise their hands. The less confident students would simply cheer, "Come on, goooooo!"

Once most of them were engaged and trying, I would acquiesce and announce, "Let's go." Students would toss their journals into the cardboard boxes by the door, a few hurling them as if attempting three-pointer shots. They'd push in chairs, ready their cash, jackets, and backpacks, and line up at the door. The frenzy usually took less than two minutes, but for me time drifted into slow motion. And it was during those slow-moving minutes that I might start to regret considering such a foray. *There's no way to make it there and back in twenty-five minutes,* I'd say to myself. And since I hadn't collected permission slips, there were legal ramifications to consider. I berated myself regularly for not being like other teachers and adhering more strictly to rules. *Permission slips are easy enough,* I could hear them saying. My response to that: *Yeah, right. Permission slips require a lot of time and paperwork.* Besides, any pre-arrangements locked us into going, eliminating the element of suspense. Around this time, my thoughts would intensify. I'd fall into a kind of dizziness. I'd lean on the door, purposefully blocking it, and wait for calm among my students (and in myself).

It was at this precise point one Friday morning in March that I happened to notice Joaquín. He was a solitary statue in a sea of swarming bodies. His huge brown eyes peered at me like full moons, and when our gazes met he looked quickly at his feet, adorned in thatched sandals. It was barely sixty degrees outside. Joaquín had arrived from the tropical Mexican state of Campeche only a week before. Not yet attuned to the local weather or where we were going, he knew only to bring money to school this day. Awkwardly he folded and unfolded the two dollars he held in his hand. Avoiding more eye contact, he stared straight ahead at the metal door in front of him, so eager for it to open onto the world beyond his bus stop and the school grounds and his apartment complex.

My self-doubt eased up. Joaquín was why the class was going to the candy store. He probably had never set foot on South Congress Avenue, probably didn't know he lived in the capital city of Texas or that the State Capitol was down that avenue and fairly close to our school. I smiled at his serious face, which again made him feel uncomfortable. He stopped fidgeting with his money and hid it in his pocket. *Kids should get time to explore*, I thought, *especially when they're from another country.* Joaquín needed a frame of reference for where he currently was in the world. I embarked on our adventure with renewed vigor.

Students, now ready, noticed me with my back to the door and arms crossed.

"Sh! Ms. Smith waiting. . . . Guys, we have only like twenty minute. Be quiet!" Magaly had taken it upon herself to herd the group. Lots of hushing. I began my safety procedures review, reminding students to stay behind me, demonstrating how to check for cars before crossing the street.

"Ms. Smith, we already know that!"

"You say that last time!"

"Let's go. Is eleven and two minute!"

"Only twenty-three minute before the bell," a mathematically inclined student shouted.

Filing out of the portable, down the wooden ramp, and onto the adjoining side street was always tricky. We had to avoid being seen by administrators or by P.E. students outdoors who might report us or, worse, try to join us. Once we'd gotten across the forty yards to the fence around the school without being sighted, we were officially on our way.

The next few residential streets provided safe passage since not many cars passed. A driver or two gave us a friendly honk. Yet soon we again entered dangerous territory, a busy two-lane street with a minuscule sidewalk, the only buffer from cars speeding by inches away. I envisioned my sixth-grade boys darting, chasing, and pushing. I hugged the curb, forcing the traffic to slow down. The sidewalk ended at South Congress Avenue, six lanes wide, two of them for bicycles. We waited there for the pedestrian crossing light.

Because the intersection was so busy, we were forced to vie for space. I noticed a few legs precariously dangling

220

off the curb as cars and bicycles whizzed by, their operators unaware. A bit panicked, I faced the students. "Back. Back. Back from the street," I yelled, arms waving.

The white stick figure lit up and urged us to cross in front of three lanes of traffic on either side that had barely come to a stop. I had no choice but to trust the universe. Numbers blinked in descending order, warning us of the seconds remaining to reach the safety of the opposite sidewalk. I prayed that no administrator was waiting at the stoplight, on her way back to the campus from a downtown meeting. *I could lose my job over this.*

Once, on a whim, in hopes of receiving retroactive permission from the powers that be, I confessed to my favorite administrator that I took my students on outings to the candy store.

"Ms. Smith," the administrator said, "don't tell me that! I did *not* hear you say that to me!" Still, I swear that when she turned to leave I heard her chuckle.

During many of our walks to the store, I had to convince myself I was doing the right thing. I gave pep talks in my head loosely titled "My Students Deserve Some Fun." They spent seven undoubtedly exhausting hours a day hearing a language largely incomprehensible. (My ESL classes provided the only instruction tailored specifically to them.) And while being taught in that incomprehensible language, they were expected to learn about graphs and angles, weights and pulleys, laws and battles. They understood maybe 20 percent of the instruction. (I tried not to think about how they struggled in those classes. What if I had to learn about Manifest Destiny in Arabic?) Despite these barriers, administrators and government officials wondered why the dropout rate among ESL learners was so high.

In many American universities, foreign students were accepted for enrollment despite insufficient English proficiency, as long as they took an intensive semester-long course in English and passed an exam, the Test of English as a Foreign Language (TOEFL), before beginning their degree-plan course load. It baffled me why my students weren't granted the same practices and reasonable guidelines. Worse, they had few advocates working to rectify their situation.

I watched as my students now pranced across the intersection like reindeer, in various clumps and oblivious of my feelings of inadequacy: *If I were a stronger disciplinarian, I wouldn't have to resort to such extreme rewards to motivate students. If I weren't such a slacker teacher, I wouldn't feel as stuck in the classroom as my students—and needing the break more than they did.*

We all made the crossing safely. As they went ahead of me down the sidewalk, three abreast and chattering loudly, I imagined my empty portable. What if some administrators walked in for an unannounced visit? The room would be infused with an eerie feeling left by the sudden departure of its occupants, just like in the folklore of mysteriously abandoned ships on the high seas. Confused, they'd search for us in the adjoining classroom. There they would find Miguel Ángel gaming away on the computer because I'd let him convince me to trade computer time for candy. One of them would whisper in my student's ear, "Where's Ms. Smith? And the rest of the class. And why aren't you with them?"

Miguel Ángel would no doubt mutter, "The candy store. But I want stay here."

"What candy store?" the administrator would ask.

"There," he'd reply then lead all of them to the small window that offered a direct view of the street. I imagined them peering out right in time to see the whole lot of us returning from our secret adventure, careening from too much sugar, sweets spilling from pockets and fists.

My fantasy concluded, I checked my watch. We'd arrived at 11:06. Yet, as occasionally happened, the glass doors were still locked. "What? Closed? But is eleven already," one of the students exclaimed in dismay. They operated in the world of school time where everything ran bell to bell.

But a minute later the young manager opened the door for us, familiar customers by now. Pretending not to notice his irritated expression—directed at me for not calling ahead of time—we brushed past him. After backpacks were tossed in the alcove that bordered the large front windows, we hightailed it to the back, where plastic bins filled with the $2.27-per-pound candy awaited us. My students' conversations were noticeably livelier today, just as more cash than usual had circulated back at the portable a short time ago. The reason for both? It was the last day before spring break. Anticipation was high not only for sweets, but for freedom and warmer weather as well.

"Quickly, quickly!" I called, herding the kids closer to me. "I need your attention!" Mainly for the benefit of the newest student, Joaquín, I delivered the candy selection instructions. Like a flight attendant demonstrating a plane's safety features, I grabbed the nearest red scoop attached to a cord and showed how to take candy out. "No hands," I warned, waving mine above my head for added effect. I tried to keep it brief, aware that I was holding court in the middle of the shop, not wanting to annoy the few other customers. I concluded by tearing a plastic bag from the roll and showing that a fistful of candy generally weighed in at one dollar's worth. This was important for kids whose eyes were larger than the amount of money in their pockets.

Throughout all of this, Joaquín had intently followed my movements, his furrowed brow telling me he was trying desperately to comprehend.

"Okay. You can get your candy now. You have four minutes," I announced.

They worked at a hectic pace, wasting no time. I stepped aside and smiled, gratified by my students' unsolicited cooperation with each other.

Their selections made, they got in line to weigh and pay. As on other trips, our checkout amazed me. We were a large group that paid individually. Many students didn't understand the cashier's English, nor did they have a solid grasp of the currency. Two kids had bought too much candy, which interrupted the flow when they needed to borrow cash from a classmate. A few others lacked money, and the cashier had to put their bags of candy to the side for me to pay for them. All these limitations could have created major holdups, but they didn't.

I observed as Joaquín, third in line, copied Victor, who stood ahead of him. Joaquín stretched his arm up to the scale but couldn't reach. Victor politely turned around, took Joaquín's bag of candy, and rested it on the stainless-steel plate. "How much?" Victor asked the cashier.

"Two-fifty," she said.

"Dos cincuenta," Victor translated for Joaquín, then counted out the amount from the money in Joaquín's palm and the transaction was done.

I stood by the counter, so enamored of my students for their attentiveness and so grateful to the two employees for their patience and flexibility. Once again, seeing my students in the community and that community being so accommodating turned out to be the high point of my week.

Then, on this Friday before spring break, something else totally unexpected happened that added to the excitement of it all. A tall man, possibly Mexican American, had appeared next to the cashier as she rang up our purchases. He carried on a friendly, relaxed banter with the employees. I assumed from the casual nature of their interaction that he was either the owner or a loyal customer. Each time a student timidly stepped up to hand over payment, the stranger calmly extended his palm as if to say, *I've got this. Keep your money.* Students hesitated and looked to me for direction. When I nodded my head to the first few, they in turn gave a sheepish nod of thanks to the tall stranger as they walked away with their bag of candy. The rest of the students followed suit. Then it was my turn to consolidate all unpaid items. *Surely, this man isn't going to include the teacher's, the only adult's, portion of the bill.* Yet the palm went up for me too, silently commanding obedience. I smiled and expressed my gratitude.

Feeling overwhelmed by such generosity but also rushed, I chose the simplest path: to press on. We congregated at the front and gathered belongings. The hubbub subsided as eating candy became the major distraction. But we sensed the clock ticking—and none of us wanted to lose sight of our worthy goal of making it to the candy store without mishap and returning with no one marked tardy for fourth period.

We spilled out the entrance into the luminous sunshine, the sky a piercing blue, the cool wind on our faces. Only four hours to go and spring break would begin. We had our candy. What's more, it was free candy so we still had money in our pockets. We'd done it again: we'd gotten away with the near impossible.

We were almost to the finish line. Fifty seconds left and only two blocks to go. We broke into a sprint. Even the stragglers tried to keep up. We were running . . . holding our bags of candy up in the air like torches . . . shrieking with joy . . . sucking Jolly Ranchers and lollipops . . . driving forward into gusts of fresh air . . . laughing . . . whooping . . . cracking up at each other's missteps . . . pointing . . . swirling . . . holding our sides that cramped from running and eating at the same time. *This is the best bonding experience of the year. We're in this together. Just us. Nobody else is having the fun we're having. My students will never forget this.*

I felt all my seemingly appropriate concerns for safety and for the most valuable use of instructional time fade away. Looking at the clusters of students behind me, I saw that while candies were bartered and exchanged, new pairs had formed, that new connections had been established.

We reached the school's iron gate by the street, then

moved into single file to follow the zigzag course of the fence. The tardy bell sounded and we sprinted a second time across the green soccer fields into the shadows of the school buildings. Some students turned toward me to wave. Others waved with their backs to me, running off to their next class or the cafeteria.

"Bye, Miss," shouted Sergio.

"See you Monday," yelled Ana, forgetting there were no classes next week.

After the last shopper had disappeared, I slipped into my portable, where lunch and solitude awaited me. Overcome by the dimness and by my ears ringing from the quiet, I slumped into my desk chair. I briefly wondered how many more of such outings I could muster. But it was Friday and the eve of a vacation. The next candy store outing lay in the distant future. I put my arms on the desk and dropped my head into the cradle they made. My precious alone time would last only ten minutes. Soon a few students would be knocking at the door, then filing in with their cafeteria trays. Sympathetic to their desire to eat in a more intimate setting than the huge, sterile, and noisy cafeteria, I could never refuse them.

I rested, but within minutes the knowledge of exactly what I'd teach the week after the break came plainly into view. My students would write thank-you letters to the man who had paid for our candy. A golden opportunity to practice true-to-life writing made me look forward to returning.

Later that afternoon I called and got the stranger's name: Gustavo Moya, a good friend of the manager and a frequent customer. I asked if the students could bring handwritten letters for Mr. Moya to the store. "Yes, of course," the manager said. He assured me the letters would get delivered.

Anticipating my students' resistance to this assignment—many agonized over writing in English—I could hear their objections. "But, Miss, his name Gustavo

Moya. He speak Spanish. We need write in Spanish." Yet knowing the language battle was more than a week away, I happily blocked it from my mind.

Then, in the quiet classroom, I turned to a more interesting thought: why had Gustavo Moya treated us so kindly? I suspected that he'd been a child immigrant himself and had fully related to my students and their circumstances. The golden life lesson for them was, I hoped, that, aside from going out into the community to practice their English and math skills, they'd experienced another adult, an American, who had their back, who was kind to them for whatever reason and wanted to let them know he valued them.

I was well aware that some of my students and their families lived in fear of *La Migra*, their term for the immigration police. I knew that my students could be leery of rude and impatient gringos. My hope was that today's candy store visit would lessen their apprehension, bring them a step closer toward mingling with the "other" culture, inspire them to venture out unaccompanied by their English-speaking teacher.

And it did inspire at least one student. The first day back from spring break, Ana informed me that she'd taken her family to the Big Top Candy Shop. "My family like it very much," she said. "Maybe we go every time after the church."

I envisioned her family of six timidly making their way around the shiny see-through bins, the kids dressed in their Sunday best and helping their parents with the serving scoops, giggling at one another's blunders. Best of all, I imagined the parents' joy in getting to share such a magical place with their children.

On one of the final days of my teaching career, months after our memorable spring break jaunt to the candy store, my students drew pictures and wrote cards of farewell. Never before having left a group of kids midyear, I hadn't been sure how to say goodbye. I'd waited until the last minute to tell them I was retiring and wouldn't be returning in January after the holidays.

My students were shocked. In disbelief. Some refused to look at me. "This no right, Ms. Smith. Is mean," muttered Carolina, jaws rigid and eyes on her drawing.

Yet it was Sergio who touched my heart the most. He was one of my more advanced students. He'd also been diagnosed with Asperger syndrome, which made him reluctant to go on candy store outings because they were hectic and meant a change in environment. This is what Sergio wrote:

Ms Smith,

Please don't leave the school.

You are good teacher.

And who gonna take kids

to the candy store?

Sinceramente,

Sergio

Made in the USA
Columbia, SC
14 October 2021